Ian Coffey is a columnist for
newspaper, the 'Western Morning News'. His weekly
column offers a faith-perspective on the news.

Kim Bush has chosen a collection of these columns and
added her own choice of readings, reflections and prayers.

Text copyright © Ian Coffey and Kim Bush 2003
The authors assert the moral right
to be identified as the authors of this work

Published by
The Bible Reading Fellowship
First Floor, Elsfield Hall
15–17 Elsfield Way, Oxford OX2 8FG
ISBN 1 84101 315 3

First published 2003
10 9 8 7 6 5 4 3 2 1 0

Acknowledgments
Unless otherwise stated, scripture quotations are taken from the Holy Bible,
New International Version, copyright © 1973, 1978, 1984 by International
Bible Society, are used by permission of Hodder & Stoughton Limited. All
rights reserved. 'NIV' is a registered trademark of International Bible Society.
UK trademark number 1448790.

Extracts from the Authorized Version of the Bible (The King James Bible), the
rights in which are vested in the Crown, are reproduced by permission of the
Crown's Patentee, Cambridge University Press.

Scripture quotations from THE MESSAGE, copyright © by Eugene H. Peterson
1993, 1994, 1995. Used by permission of NavPress Publishing Group.

Scripture quotations marked (Living Water) are taken from the Holy Bible, New
Living Translation, copyright © 1996. Used by permission of Tyndale House
Publishers, Inc., Wheaton, Illinois 60189. All rights reserved.

A catalogue record for this book is available from the British Library

Printed and bound in Great Britain by
Bookmarque, Croydon

Doorways *from the* Word

to the World

Ian Coffey with Kim Bush

Contents

Doorways to Forgiveness

Doorways to Encouraging Others

Doorways to Praying the Lord's Prayer

Doorways to Prayer

Doorways to Discipleship

Introduction

Doorways are useful. They provide a way in and a way out; they are markers of boundaries. And if you stand in a doorway you get to look at what is on both sides.

Doorways are not usually noticed. There are exceptions, of course. Number 10 Downing Street must be the most photographed door in the world. But most doors we pass through each day barely merit more than a glance.

Doorways are important. They provide protection, security and the offer of a safe place.

Here is a collection of doorways. We offer them in the hope that they will open the way to a fresh understanding of God, ourselves and the world around us.

Doorways to Knowing Ourselves

Marred masterpieces

Our great God and Saviour, Jesus Christ... gave himself for us to redeem us from all wickedness and to purify for himself a people that are his very own, eager to do what is good.

TITUS 2:13–14

I wouldn't get too close if I were you. I am recovering from a virus that has disrupted my life for weeks.

I need to come clean (pun intended) and explain that, strictly speaking, it is not me who had the virus, but a special part of me. I can now announce to the world, though, that the bug has gone and life has a rosier tinge.

My home computer picked up a virus some months ago and has been happily passing it on to all and sundry. Even my little laptop got the bug. I was in blissful ignorance until I sent a floppy disc to a publisher who was not a happy bunny to discover that my virus was now trying to infect the whole of his networked system—not the best way to endear yourself to people, I quickly discovered.

The good news is that I have a friend who understands such mysteries and this week was able to kill the virus and clean up my machine.

'But where do computer viruses come from?' I asked. My friend gave me the sort of patronizing look that adults give four-year-olds when they ask the same sort of question about babies. Come to think of it, he used the same tone of voice that goes along with such parental explanations.

Apparently, there's a bunch of computer anoraks around the world who while away their time making up such viruses and sending them out to create havoc. That's right, it's an expensive techno-joke played by a few who want to mess things up for everyone else. Nice people, huh?

Why do we have an inbuilt propensity to spoil things? One of the early Christian Fathers, Athanasius, described humans as a wonderful masterpiece that has had a pot of ink thrown across it. It is ruined, but beneath the stains you can still see the glory of the original.

That comment has helped me to understand the dichotomy of human nature. (And I'm not pointing a finger, simply looking into my own heart.) How can so many good, kind and gentle things live alongside such ugly, cruel and selfish things?

We're a marred masterpiece—spoilt, but still showing the image of its Creator.

Thankfully, we don't have to gaze at the ruined painting and mourn for what could have been. The Artist himself has a unique gift of cleaning up the mess and restoring the image.

For further reading

TITUS 2:1–15

We cannot clean up the mess in our lives simply by resolving to be better and trying hard. Nor should we sit back and leave God to get on with the job. Paul explains to Titus that it is God's grace which 'teaches us to say "No" to ungodliness and worldly passions, and to live self-controlled, upright and godly lives' (v. 12) in the midst of the ungodliness that surrounds us. If God's grace teaches us, then we are called to be receptive learners. How do we learn? By taking every opportunity to do so, by studying the Bible, listening to sermons, reading helpful books, being open to the prompting and instruction of God's Holy Spirit and by being thoughtful about how we live and behave. This chapter is an exhortation by Paul to Titus to teach relevantly to different groups within the churches. There are different lessons to learn at every stage of our lives. We will never know it all, and this should keep us humble.

Prayer

Thank you, Lord Jesus, that day by day I am being transformed to become more like you as I allow you to deal with the things that mar the beauty of your image in me.

Meaninglessness

Written in September 1995 after the fourth World Conference on Women

We have this hope as an anchor for the soul, firm and secure.
HEBREWS 6:19

How much do you think you are worth? Not very much, according to this analysis of an average human being. We are made up of the following:

- Enough fat for seven bars of soap
- Enough iron for a medium-sized nail
- Enough sugar for seven cups of tea
- Enough lime to whitewash a chicken shed
- Enough phosphorus to put the tips on 2,200 matches
- Enough magnesium for a dose of salts
- Enough potash to explode a toy crane
- Enough sulphur to rid an average-sized dog of fleas

The bulk of us consists of water, so add that and the cost of the above together and you would have change from a fiver. But is that how we calculate the value of a human life?

Most of us know instinctively that we are more than a chance collection of chemicals. We find a chord echoing within when we read, 'So God created man in his own image, in the image of God he created him; male and female he created them' (Genesis 1:27).

As reports have emerged from Beijing regarding the fourth World Conference on Women, they have carried a mixed message. Despite media-speak assertions of a 'global sisterhood' developing, the conference has the appearance of a modern-day Tower of Babel. The gulf of language, culture and lifestyles between Islamic fundamentalists and Western lesbian protesters leaves many observers wondering who is paying for those 40,000 delegates to shout at each other in a country that has a record on women's rights akin to Herod the Great's on childcare.

But at the heart of this conference crucial matters have been raised that don't deserve to be lost. For example, did you know that among the world's 20 million refugees, 80 per cent are women and children? According to Amnesty International, fifteen major nations use rape as a 'weapon of war'. In Central America, where one-third of families are headed by women, 75 per cent are living beneath the poverty line.

It is a gross injustice that, in some countries, female babies are abandoned to die, and that those who live remain destined to abuse, poverty, disease and oppression.

The Chinese have an ancient proverb that says, 'How sad it is to be a woman; nothing on earth is held so cheap.' But not to the God who made them.

For further reading

ECCLESIASTES 9:1–12; 1 CORINTHIANS 15:17–20

Ecclesiastes is an uncomfortable, sometimes depressing book to read. The writer of this passage has been taking a good, hard look at people and life and has come to the conclusion that the living are only marginally better off than the dead. Life is a lottery where good people do not always get the rewards they deserve and where death can come at any time. Therefore, he concludes, we should make the most of life while we can, even though it is ultimately meaningless. If we look at the world today, at the inequalities, war and poverty, then we will have to agree with the writer of Ecclesiastes, except in one very important respect: death is not the end and life is not meaningless. We are not 'to be pitied more than all men' (1 Corinthians 15:19) because Jesus came to make a way for us to be reconciled to God. He died and rose again and because of this we too may live. And he will return to bring an end once and for all to the injustices of the world. This is our secure hope.

Prayer

Dear Lord, I often do not know how to pray for the needy world that I live in but I know that those things that sadden me bring you even greater sorrow and that no injustice passes unnoticed by you.

God's choice

Who despises the day of small things?

ZECHARIAH 4:10

Press reports that the Church of England were planning psychometric tests for those who applied to train for Christian ministry reminded me of a spoof report compiled by a team of management consultants and addressed to Jesus, advising him on his choice of disciples:

Thank you for submitting the resumés of the twelve men you have picked for management positions in your new organization. All of them have now taken our battery of tests, and we have not only run the results through our computer but also have arranged personal interviews for each of them with our psychologist and vocational aptitude consultant.

It is our opinion that most of your nominees are lacking in background, education and vocational aptitude for the type of enterprise you are undertaking. They do not have the team concept. We would recommend that you continue your search for persons of experience in managerial ability and proven capability.

Simon Peter is emotionally unstable and given to fits of temper. Andrew has absolutely no qualities of leadership. The two brothers, James and John, the sons of Zebedee, place personal interest above company loyalty. Thomas demonstrates a questioning attitude that would tend to undermine morale. We feel that it is our duty to tell you that Matthew has been blacklisted by the Greater Jerusalem Better Business Bureau. James the son of Alphaeus, and Thaddeus, definitely have radical leanings and they both registered a high score on the manic-depressive scale.

One of the candidates, however, shows great potential. He is a man of ability and resourcefulness, meets people well, has a keen business mind and has contacts in high places. He is highly motivated, ambitious and innovative. We recommend Judas Iscariot as your controller and right-hand man.

As much as I applaud attempts to be more careful in selecting potential church leaders, I am reminded that God sees things that can often be hidden by even the most sophisticated tests. After all, as the Bible spells out clearly: 'The Lord does not look at the things man looks at. Man looks at the outward appearance, but the Lord looks at the heart' (1 Samuel 16:7).

Personality analysis may provide some clues, but the ultimate test is that of character—and it takes more than a clipboard and a degree in psychology to discover that.

For further reading

ZECHARIAH 4:1–14

The Israelites had returned from exile and started to rebuild the temple despite opposition and threats from the people around them. God sent this prophecy to Zechariah to encourage him that what Zerubbabel had started, God would enable him to finish (v. 9). He was not to depend on 'might' or 'power' but on God's Spirit for protection and the ability to complete the task (v. 6).

God often surprises us by the kind of people he chooses to use in preference to the mighty and powerful: the shepherd boy who became a king; the boy whose lunch miraculously fed five thousand people; the prostitute who saved the lives of the Israelite spies; the runaway slave, Onesimus, who became 'useful' to the apostle Paul. It is inspiring to hear what God can do through people who rely not on their own resources but on his Holy Spirit. If God can use them, he can use me.

Prayer

O use me, Lord, use even me,
Just as thou wilt, and when, and where,
Until Thy blessed face I see,
Thy rest, Thy joy, Thy glory share.

FRANCES RIDLEY HAVERGAL (1836–79)

Happy to work

Written in July 2000.

We gave you this rule: 'If a man will not work, he shall not eat.'
2 THESSALONIANS 3:10

Work, according to Oscar Wilde, is the refuge of people who have nothing better to do—and according to recent research, quite a few of us would like to follow Wilde and *find* something better to do.

A joint British/American survey recently revealed only one in three Britons claims to enjoy their job. We landed seventeenth in an international league table of job satisfaction, holding bottom place for Europe. Workers claimed that long hours, the problems of commuting and insecurity about long-term employment were the biggest factors behind their dissatisfaction.

The Institute of Managers conducted a separate survey and the findings are disturbing. Eighty-seven per cent said that they had no time for interests other than work, and 71 per cent believed that their work was adversely affecting their health. The report also revealed alarmingly high figures for those managers who believed that their jobs were having an adverse effect on family life and personal relationships.

Those who study the world of work suggest that these figures are not isolated but that over a period of years, British job satisfaction has been moving steadily downwards. But why? Compared to previous generations, we have never had it so good. Is our unhappiness at work linked to a deeper root cause of dissatisfaction with life?

Let me try a quote for size: 'We enjoy a thousand material advantages over any previous generation, and yet we suffer a depth of insecurity and spiritual doubt they never knew.' These are not the words of an archbishop but of a politician. They were written by Tony Blair in 1995.

I have written a series of sermons dealing with the world of work and I've realized how much the Bible says on the subject. Job satisfaction, dealing with the public, handling harassment, being a good boss, becoming a reliable employee, developing communication skills, practising integrity—you name it and it's there.

Perhaps one reason why many of us find it hard to enjoy work is that we've forgotten what it is there for. We are meant to work in order to live, not live in order to work. And once we get those priorities the right way round, work becomes less of a chore and more of a gift.

'When God gives any man wealth and possessions, and enables him to enjoy them, to accept his lot and be happy in his work—this is a gift of God' (Ecclesiastes 5:19).

For further reading

2 THESSALONIANS 3:6–15

In the Thessalonian church, there were those who were expecting the imminent return of Jesus (or possibly were using this as a convenient excuse) and so had given up working to support themselves. Paul points out how he and his companions had 'worked night and day' so as not to 'be a burden' on the other believers and to set them an example (vv. 8–9). He tells the Thessalonians to continue to regard these 'idle' men as brothers but not to associate with them (vv. 6, 15). But what about those who are unemployed because they have no choice? It's tough having to face the discouragement and rejection as well as the practical difficulties of being unable to find work. But our value to God is not determined by our pay-slip or lack of it, or by the status of the job we do. And our self-worth should not come from these things but from knowing that we are loved and infinitely valuable to him. If he has given us this gift of 'spare time', we should try to invest it wisely in our family and friends, our church and community, and in getting to know him better.

Prayer

Thank God for the gift of work. Pray for anyone you know who is unemployed and finding it tough, that God would use this time to bless them and that they would be encouraged along the way as they look for work.

The sky at night

What is man that you are mindful of him, the son of man that you
care for him?

PSALM 8:4

In his bestselling book, *A Brief History of Time* (Bantam Press, 1989), the
British physicist Stephen Hawking cuts us all down to size with his
description of Earth as 'a medium size planet orbiting around an average
star in the outer suburbs of an ordinary spiral galaxy, which is itself only
one of about a million million galaxies in the observable universe'.

The Milky Way, described by Hawking as 'an ordinary spiral galaxy',
measures 621,000 million million miles across and contains about
100,000 million stars. As mind-stretching as it may sound, ours is one
galaxy among millions of others.

One writer tries to put it into perspective with this description: if we
could travel at the speed of light (which is 186,282 miles per second)
we could reach the moon in 1.3 seconds and the sun in 8.3 minutes.
But at the same speed it would take four years to reach the Milky Way,
and some astronomers have identified galaxies that are millions of light
years away. In 1996 the Hubble space telescope found six massive
objects that appear to be fourteen billion light years away.

All of this underlines a truth and raises a question. The truth is that
we are unbelievably tiny within the vastness of the universe. And the
question is, what is it all for?

Often the sheer pace and busyness of life mean that we have neither
time nor energy to stop and think. But life throws up some landmark
moments when the passing of time is noted—a birth, a death, a marriage
or separation. Such moments provide the opportunity for reflection and,
in the words of a friend, we get to lift our heads from the trough for a
few moments and look up.

King David wrote some profound God-thoughts. In one of his psalms he asks the question, 'When I consider your heavens, the work of your fingers, the moon and the stars, which you have set in place, what is man that you are mindful of him, the son of man that you care for him?' (Psalm 8:3–4).

As David concludes, God has given human beings a unique place within the vastness of his creation. We are made by him and for him, and until we know him we have not begun to live.

Tiny? Yes. Insignificant? No.

For further reading

PSALM 8:1–9; JOB 7:17–21

Psalm 8 evokes a picture of David walking out on a peaceful night and gazing up at a star-filled sky. As his thoughts turn towards the majesty of God displayed in creation, he is moved to wonder that God should care for men and women and give us such a high place in the order of things. Job's words almost echo David's (v.17). David surveyed creation and his own place in it, and his words poured out in praise. Job, however, was wrestling with hard questions about his own terrible physical suffering, bereavement and loss, and his words were words of complaint. Life's big events and changes challenge us. Sometimes praise flows naturally as we marvel at God's goodness to us. At other times we may be tempted to feel that God has abandoned us or turned against us. It isn't so. He had not abandoned Job and he brought him gradually to the place where he was ready to give God a hearing. God was 'mindful' of Job and he is 'mindful' of us. Whatever our life's circumstances, his love does not falter.

Prayer

Do you identify more with Job or with David right now? Thank God that he is 'mindful' of you and never stops loving you.

How does God see me?

But if we judged ourselves, we would not come under judgment.

1 CORINTHIANS 11:31

Imagine the shock of reading the paper over breakfast and discovering your own obituary. It happened in 1888 to Alfred Nobel, the Swedish chemist and industrialist. Owing to a mix-up at the newspaper office, journalists confused Alfred with his brother and ran the wrong obituary. Apart from the shock, he experienced acute embarrassment that ultimately led him to a change of direction in his life.

Nobel was a complex, lonely man, who achieved fame through a mixture of brilliance and business acumen. As an explosives expert, he invented a safe and manageable form of nitro-glycerine in 1866 and christened it 'dynamite'. He went on to patent other discoveries in the field of explosives and built an empire of 80 companies in 20 different countries to handle his interests, which made him a wealthy man.

But the mistaken obituary caused him great concern as, for the first time, he saw how the world would remember him. He had developed explosives primarily for use in mining and road construction but the obituary portrayed him as making his fortune from the misfortune of war. He saw himself as others saw him—an industrialist who traded in armaments and made money from human misery.

This led to a change in the direction of his life. He altered the terms of his will to show a different face to the world. He had high ideals for peace and progress and wanted to demonstrate in a tangible way his concern for humanity.

When Nobel died in 1896, the bulk of his fortune was left to endow annual prizes for those who had made the most significant contribution in each of five areas—physics, chemistry, medicine, literature and peace. Instructions were left as to how the prizes would be awarded each year, and to the present day they remain prestigious.

Perhaps the best-known is the Nobel Peace Prize which has an illustrious list of recipients. It is strange that Nobel's name today is most strongly associated with peace when the premature obituary linked him with war. His decision to change direction paid off and left the world with a better and happier memory of him.

Alfred Nobel was 55 when he read his premature death notice, and he lived another eight years—which reminds us that it is never impossible or too late to change direction.

Anyone for a conversion?

For further reading

COLOSSIANS 4:7–18

Paul often closed his letters with greetings from his fellow workers and messages to individuals within the churches. In a few words we are given brief glimpses into the lives of these otherwise unknown people who lived and served God so long ago. Sadly, we learn that Demas, who is mentioned here (v. 14), later deserted Paul (2 Timothy 4:10). We know from the letter to Philemon that Onesimus, the 'faithful and dear brother' was once a runaway slave, and Archippus is also mentioned there. It's a shame that Euodia and Syntyche are remembered today mainly for their falling out with each other and not for the commendable work they had done in the past and possibly went on to do (Philippians 4:2–3). Our lives may not be recorded for people to read about generations later, but if we were to ask ourselves, 'What does God think about the way I am living right now?' what would our answer be?

Prayer

Heavenly Father, there are times when I would like to hide the way I am living from you because I know it grieves you. I am so glad that when I come to my senses you are there to forgive and welcome me.

Reflections

Let us fix our eyes on Jesus.

HEBREWS 12:2

If you had to pick something that summed up the 20th century, what would you choose?

It is not as daft a question as it sounds. The new Museum of Scotland has been asking the great and famous for their selections. Prime Minister Tony Blair has opted for the Fender Stratocaster electric guitar and although I appreciate his good taste I'm not sure how many would agree.

It's a fascinating question. If you face a social occasion this weekend where the conversation seems likely to flag, try tossing it in and listening to the different answers!

For my part, I would like to suggest a mirror as the object that sums up the century. Rarely has there been a period in history when we have been so preoccupied with ourselves.

Change has accelerated with the pedal flat on the floor. We have seen two World Wars and innumerable other conflicts. We have seen enormous advances in science and technology. We have walked on the surface of the moon and discovered how to create life in a test tube. The world has become a global village that we traverse with ease, and yet poverty, injustice and disease continue to blight the lives of millions. The 20th century certainly tells a mixed story.

My choice of a mirror as its symbol stems from a belief that, in spite of all our achievements, we have lost what is sometimes called 'a sense of the transcendent'. Put simply, we have left God out of the picture.

A few days ago I stood with a friend under a magnificent, clear sky and gazed at the stars. As an amateur astronomer, he delighted in showing off his knowledge by giving me a guided tour of the night sky.

It reminded me of President Roosevelt's friendship with the naturalist,

William Beebe. The two would often stand under the stars, locate a tiny patch of light near the constellation of Pegasus and recite together, 'That is the spiral galaxy in Andromeda. It is as large as our Milky Way. It is one of a hundred million galaxies. It consists of one hundred billion suns, each larger than our own sun.' After a pause, Roosevelt would add, 'Now I think we are small enough. Let's go to bed!'

More time reflecting and less time looking at our own reflections might lead to a clearer picture of our true size.

For further reading

HEBREWS 12:1–13; ROMANS 12:1–3

It is sad that a mirror should be an appropriate symbol of how we have lived in the 20th century when it is the cross of Christ that is the focal point of all history and the death of Christ that can make all the difference to the past, the future and to us right now. If we spend all our time preoccupied with ourselves, we will never change or make progress. It is only by fixing our eyes on Jesus that we are transformed. The writer to the Hebrews portrays the Christian life as a race. No one can run a race while looking in a mirror! Instead, as the hymn writer put it, 'Christ is the path and Christ the prize' and we need to keep our eyes focused on him. If we look only at ourselves and what we can do in our own strength, we will soon 'grow weary and lose heart' (v. 3). We should think of ourselves 'with sober judgment' (Romans 12:3), realizing that although we may be very, very small and unimportant, yet at the same time we matter infinitely to God.

Prayer

Lord Jesus, I don't want to 'conform… to the pattern of this world' (Romans 12:2) and live by its standards. I want to keep my eyes fixed on you.

Doorways to Knowing God

God's justice

Written October 2000, when parts of the UK were hit by severe floods

God made him who had no sin to be sin for us, so that in him we might become the righteousness of God.

2 CORINTHIANS 5:21

Are the recent floods a sign of God's judgment? I ask for two reasons. First, I received this week a copy letter and petition addressed to Prince Charles, urging him to call a national day of prayer in the light of the flooding that has wreaked havoc in so many parts of Britain. Second, a press report revealed that a leading African politician claims that the floods are a direct sign of divine displeasure.

President Taylor of Liberia gave an interview in Paris this week and accused Britain of fomenting civil war in Sierra Leone in order to steal the nation's diamonds. He declared, 'The British have managed to stop European aid to Liberia. But I am a Christian and God sent floods to Britain that will cost $1–2 billion. God punished Britain.'

What can we make of all this? I have no problem with a day of prayer for the nation; we could do with all the help we can get. I also believe that many aspects of our national life are far from what they should be. We need the sort of radical change that only comes from above. But I feel decidedly uneasy about pigeon-holing natural disasters as simply 'acts of God'—irrespective of how the insurance companies phrase their policies.

The Bible has many examples of God moving in judgment against nations, often on the grounds of their callous treatment of other people. Try reading through the opening chapters of the prophet Amos and you'll see what I mean.

But leaping to rash conclusions stirs up more questions than answers. For example, are all natural disasters to be read as punishments? If so, then it would seem that a lot of innocent people are punished wrongly and a large number of guilty ones get away scot-free. In such a scenario, heaven's justice would not appear very just.

As a number of experts have suggested, recent weather patterns could be linked to our misuse of the environment. Similarly, flood defences cost money and we now face a bigger bill for repairs as a result of choosing not to pay a more modest bill to protect ourselves.

These are choices we have made, and choices have consequences. This would appear to be a judgment we have brought on ourselves, rather than one handed down from on high.

For further reading

EZEKIEL 14:12–23

In this passage God addresses the question: how can a just God allow suffering? His judgment is about to fall on Israel and he says that even if the three spiritual giants, Noah, Daniel and Job, were there, 'they could save only themselves by their righteousness' (v. 14); the people would die for their own sins. We are sinners who have rebelled against God and do not deserve his love and mercy. Only Jesus has lived a completely righteous life (Hebrews 4:15) and when we face the ultimate disaster, eternity separated from God, only if we are depending on his righteousness will we be spared. God told Ezekiel that although he might question God's justice now, when he met the survivors of the disaster he would see that God had behaved justly. In a similar way, at the end of time, when we see things as they truly are, we too will be able to see the proof of what we believe by faith now, that God *never* acts unjustly.

Prayer

Holy God, I deserve your judgment, not your mercy and I thank you for your great love that would rather pay the price yourself than treat me as I deserve.

The Incarnation Project

'For my thoughts are not your thoughts, neither are your ways my ways,' declares the Lord.
ISAIAH 55:8

Ladies and Gentlemen, we need to draw matters to a conclusion on this Performance Management Review. I think we are all united in our views, but let me recap for the record.

The subject of our review—the Grand Designer—has fallen far short of our expectations through 'The Incarnation Project'. The whole thing has been a dismal failure.

In the Preparation category we have scored a low two, as a bunch of Old Testament prophecies hardly added to the build-up normally associated with a successful advertising campaign. The fact that the majority of religious leaders failed to recognize the Son of God on earth supports our findings.

The Presentation section was equally dismal—no feel of anything grand at all. To choose an out-of-the-way nation, centuries before the dawn of the technological age, shows a distinct lack of judgment. A stable filled with animals, a few scruffy shepherds and some very dodgy 'new age types' is not the stuff of TV spectaculars. Three out of ten, I think.

On the Communication front, I think we all agree that this rates a one—and only just. 'An all-round flop' is our corporate conclusion. After all, this is the Grand Designer's specialist area, having invented the capacity to think and communicate. All this 'In the beginning was the Word, and the Word was with God, and the Word was God'. What does that mean to your average consumer? What is lacking is the crisp soundbite that really sells or the catchy tune that won't leave you alone. Most disappointing.

So adding the scores together gives a total of six out of a possible 30 points, which, under our PMR guidelines, means a fail and a re-sit.

How anyone in their right mind could imagine that this could change the world beats me! I note from the Projected Outcomes section that the candidate mentions millions of people affected over a 2000-year period, buildings packed with worshippers celebrating the great event and every nation on earth being represented.

Well, pardon my cynicism, but pigs might fly. If anyone thinks about this sorry little performance for more than a few weeks, we'd all be most surprised.

For this Incarnation Project to take off would take nothing short of a miracle—and a pretty big one at that.

For further reading

1 CORINTHIANS 1:18–31

Have you ever been ridiculed for the things that you believe, or feared to speak out because you thought you would not be taken seriously? It is not the sophisticated way in which we present the good news about Jesus that draws men and women to him but the simple truth that he loves them and died on the cross for them. We live at a time when presentation is often seen to be more important than actual facts. But God is not going to fill our churches because we use the right techniques. Although we need to be culturally relevant to the people we are trying to reach for Jesus we should not become over-dependent on the kind of methods that see everything as a product to be sold. The apostle Paul did not compromise his preaching to appeal to the Jews who would have preferred 'miraculous signs' rather than a Messiah dying like a criminal, or to the Greeks who would have liked a more 'intellectually respectable' means of salvation. We also need to be careful that we don't rewrite the good news about Jesus because we think our message will then be more appealing. The good news has a power all of its own (Romans 1:16).

Prayer

Think about what Paul meant when he said, 'I have become all things to all men so that by all possible means I might save some' (1 Corinthians 9:22) and ask God what it should mean for you.

Counting the femtoseconds

With the Lord a day is like a thousand years, and a thousand years
are like a day.
2 Peter 3:8

I have just found a brand new word and I desperately want to try it out.
So here goes. 'Femtosecond.' That's it. I feel better already.

Now you are probably wondering what I'm talking about, so I'd better
explain. A femtosecond is the smallest unit of time and is measured as
a quadrillionth of a second. In fact, it is to a second what a second is to
32 million years. 'Wow!' I hear you gasp.

I discovered this amazing piece of information only this week, as I
read that American scientists have developed the world's most accurate
clock, which measures time to a millionth of a billionth of a second. It
may not bring the price of bacon down but the discovery is hailed as a
major breakthrough for global communications, so watch this space.

Time and its passing have fascinated human beings since—well, ever
since human beings began. I wonder why?

Milan Cathedral boasts three magnificent archways as an entrance,
each with an inscription above. The first shows a wreath of roses and the
words, 'All that pleases is but for a moment.' The second features a cross
and the inscription, 'All that troubles is but for a moment.' The third
entrance at the centre, leading to the main aisle, has above the archway
the words, 'That only is important which is eternal.'

Visitors to the cathedral are reminded that pleasure and pain may
pass but our priorities should always be shaped with eternity in view.

In what is thought to be the oldest psalm in the Bible, Moses, the
man God used to lead the nation of Israel for 40 years, engages in some
heavy-duty thinking about time and eternity. Having reflected that God
lives outside of time and yet has placed human beings to live within

its confining boundaries, he makes the following heartfelt prayer:

'Teach us to number our days aright, that we may gain a heart of wisdom… May the favour of the Lord our God rest upon us; establish the work of our hands for us' (Psalm 90:12, 17).

I like this thought from a writer called Babatunde Olatunji: 'Yesterday is history. Tomorrow is a mystery. And today? Today is a gift. That's why we call it the present.'

And it's a present where even the femtoseconds count.

For further reading

2 PETER 3:1–18

Scientists have their own ways of measuring time but Peter says that God regards time quite differently. He was writing to believers who were becoming discouraged by the taunts of people who said that since Jesus was taking so long about returning, it was doubtful that it was ever going to happen. What they had deliberately forgotten, Peter said, was that the destruction that will occur on 'the day of the Lord' (v. 10) had already happened once in history, when God had destroyed the world with a flood and only Noah and his family had been saved. If we have become comfortable with the fact that Jesus has not returned yet, we may need to rekindle the sense of expectation of Jesus' imminent return that the early believers had, so that we can take advantage of God's patience, not only to make sure we need not be ashamed of our own lives (v. 14) but also to encourage and help others to 'come to repentance' (v. 9).

Prayer

Give me a faithful heart,
Likeness to Thee,
That each departing day
Henceforth may see
Some work of love begun,
Some deed of kindness done,
Some wanderer sought and won—
Something for Thee.

SYLVANUS DRYDEN PHELPS (1816–95)

Doorways to Worship

Music in church

May the peoples praise you, O God; may all the peoples praise you.
Psalm 67:3

One subject that is guaranteed to get most Christians hot and bothered is music in church. Forget Third World debt, the ordination of women, racism or the repeal of Section 28, if you want hackles to rise and fur to fly, try changing the hymn book.

A friend sent me a story that illustrates the size of the gulf when it comes to tastes in Christian music.

A farmer visited a big city church and, on his return home, his wife asked what differences he had noticed compared to their village chapel. He gave a long list. 'What about the music?' she asked. 'They seem to sing more modern worship songs than hymns,' he told her. She couldn't understand the difference so he offered the following explanation.

'Well, if I were to say to you, "Martha, the cows are in the corn," that would be a hymn. But if I said, "Martha, Martha, Martha, ooh Martha, the cows, the big cows, the black cows, the brown cows, the white cows, all the cows, cows, cows are in the corn, are in the corn, are in the corn," that would be a modern worship song.'

Now depending on whether you are deeply offended by that story or are now falling about laughing and wondering who you can cut this out and send it to, I can predict which side of 1945 you were born.

Music, like so many things, comes down to personal taste, and factors such as culture, temperament and upbringing affect our taste. But we get into dangerous territory when we claim that one type of Christian music is more spiritual than another.

What did Jesus have to say about worship? From what we can gather, attitude of heart seemed higher up his priority list than any music style. 'Your worship must engage your spirit in the pursuit of truth. That's the kind of people the Father is out looking for: those who are simply and honestly *themselves* before him in their worship' (John 4:23, THE MESSAGE).

On that basis, musical styles ranging from pipe organs to bongo drums get a look in. Music becomes a vehicle to express what is in the heart of people offering a priceless gift to God.

Think of worship as a neatly parcelled present. The wrapping plays a part but it is not the gift itself. It's what's inside that counts.

For further reading

PSALM 113:1–9

Authentic worship is about pleasing God. The fact that it blesses us is a by-product, not its aim. When Paul says that offering our bodies as 'living sacrifices' is our 'spiritual act of worship' (Romans 12:1), he is saying that our physical lives, as well as our hearts and minds, are part of our worship. What we do when we come together as the body of Christ should be the overspill from the rest of our life, not an isolated activity. Worship is not something that can be timetabled into our lives; it's a full-time occupation. God has made each one of us unique and when we do come together, our worship should be inclusive. What kind of worshippers are we if we sulk when we don't get to sing from our favourite hymn book or when we criticize what blesses others but may not bless us? Surely God is pleased when we are glad that others are able to worship him in a way that relates to them. And no matter how beautifully we sing and express ourselves, if we come with unconfessed sin or a preoccupied mind, our worship will not please God. Worship isn't worship if it's all about me.

Prayer

Jesus! My Shepherd, Saviour, Friend,
My Prophet, Priest and King,
My Lord, my Life, my Way, my End,
Accept the praise I bring.

JOHN NEWTON (1725–1807)

Keep in touch

Come near to God and he will come near to you.
JAMES 4:8

I have nothing against Mr Bell personally. I am sure he was a wonderful man and a great joy to his parents. But I confess I hold him responsible for a great deal of hassle in my life.

I am referring to the Mr Bell with the forenames Alexander Graham. He is best remembered as the Scotsman who moved to America and invented the telephone. On 5 June 1875 he placed a call to his assistant and, according to history, a modern labour-saving device was given to the world.

That's where my problem with him begins. There are times when his invention is a great blessing and, for many people, a vital means of staying in touch. But, on the down side, the telephone is one of the greatest causes of conflict in my life.

For example, have you noticed how it always rings when you are about to eat a meal? Or how it summons you from the shower, down three flights of stairs, only to stop ringing once you arrive, dripping wet, in the kitchen? Also, it has an abnormal relationship with teenagers. In my house they can't hear it ring when it is just three feet from their elbow. But when they do pick it up, invisible superglue seeps out, leaving them attached for up to two hours at a time.

My frustration with Mr Bell's invention recently reached a new peak. Having rung a company to pose them a small query, I was routed through an elaborate system of answer machines demanding that I press buttons to identify my need. I was then put on hold for a 'customer operative to deal with you personally'. After ten minutes of 'round the mulberry bush' my question was answered in less than 60 seconds. Isn't technology wonderful?

With less-than-charitable thoughts in my heart towards Mr Bell and the world in general, I came across these words in the Old Testament: 'Call to me and I will answer you and tell you great and unsearchable things you do not know' (Jeremiah 33:3). At a time of national chaos and uncertainty, God promises to give Jeremiah straight answers to honest questions.

We spend so much on communications and yet seem to have lost the art of communicating. Not so with God who, according to this verse, makes an offer not even BT could match.

For further reading

Isaiah 55:1–7

What a beautiful promise this is from James: 'Come near to God and he will come near to you.' Our creator has the right to demand our attention but he does not force himself upon us; he waits for us to invite him. How amazing it is that almighty God should not only have time to spare for us but should put no limits on how much time he gives us. It is we who do that, allocating God an hour or two on a Sunday, a little time during the week, perhaps scarcely giving him a thought at other times, and yet as soon as we draw near to him he is there, forgiving, loving and blessing us (v. 7). How careless we are, at times, of this immense privilege. How freely he gives to us, demanding nothing in return (vv. 1–2). He turns no one away. Isaiah says, 'Seek the Lord while he may be found; call on him while he is near' (v. 6). So let's do that, with thankfulness.

Prayer

Father, I thank you that you are right here with me now. I draw near to you in confidence that you will not turn me away. Thank you, Lord.

Praise the Lord!

Written in March 1999.

Sing joyfully to the Lord, you righteous; it is fitting for the upright to praise him.

PSALM 33:1

With the news dominated by the Budget this week, my mind is reeling with what can only be described as the paralysis of analysis. During a long car journey on Tuesday, I tuned in to most of the Chancellor's long speech and on the return trip was treated to the experts debating the vital question, 'Who gets what?'

It was refreshing the next morning to turn from pages of newsprint on the subject to discover a cutting I had filed a few months back. It was a letter to the editor of *The Evening Standard*, written by the actress, Helen Mirren.

Dear Sir,

I was at a Unicef Champion Children's award lunch on Friday, celebrating the achievements of a group of kids under the age of sixteen. It was an occasion of many heart-warming stories and the one I want to share came from Donna, a community worker from Sheffield. She was with the family of a winner, Jake Bonsall, from a particularly tough estate in Sheffield.

They had a couple of hours to spend to see some of London but, not having been here before, didn't know where to start. Donna hailed a black cab and said, 'We've got £20—that's all we can spend. Take us to see as much of London as we can for the money. Don't skank us, because that's all we've got.'

The family set off, watching the meter nervously. After a couple of minutes, the cabbie switched the meter off and took them on a two-hour excursion round

London—from Fleet Street to Buckingham Palace, from the Tower to Princess Diana's favourite restaurant. That cabbie did the most wonderful thing for the Bonsall family, for Londoners and for the London Cab Service. I salute him and wish his kindness to be known to a greater public. Thank you, whoever you are—if there was an award ceremony for brilliant cabbies, you would be my nomination.

Helen Mirren, c/o Royal National Theatre

Jesus said, 'Watch out! Be on your guard against all kinds of greed; a man's life does not consist in the abundance of his possessions' (Luke 12:15).

At times we seem obsessed about getting rather than giving. Thank goodness Comic Relief Day came along on Friday and helped put the Budget in a new light. After all, generosity is inflation-proof, tax-free and the long-term benefits are out of this world.

For further reading

PSALM 33:1–22

The book of Psalms is so encouraging. Here we find writers who wrestled with the same sort of problems as we do. The Psalms are an invitation to us to come before God as we are, to lay our difficulties before the one who knows us better than we know ourselves (v. 15) and still loves us, and ask for his help. But not every day is a struggle. Sometimes our hearts are uplifted by a story of unselfishness and generosity like the one Helen Mirren told. Or we may receive good news, or something unexpected and pleasant may happen to us. Those are days when praising God is the most natural and joyous thing to do. Psalm 33 is one in which the dominant theme is praise and the focus is on God, not us. We can thank God for his goodness that underpins our lives, for the encouragements he gives us along the way, for the kindness and generosity of others, and for the many blessings that we too often take for granted. 'In him our hearts rejoice, for we trust in his holy name' (v. 21).

Prayer

Praise God from whom all blessings flow,
Praise him, all creatures here below;
Praise him above, ye heavenly host,
Praise Father, Son and Holy Ghost.

THOMAS KEN (1637–1711)

Doorways to Christian Character

But the fruit of the Spirit is love, joy, peace, patience, kindness, goodness, faithfulness, gentleness and self-control. Against such things there is no law.
(Galatians 5:22–23)

Love

But God demonstrates his own love for us in this: While we were still sinners, Christ died for us.

ROMANS 5:8

Richard Selzer is a surgeon who has written a book entitled *Mortal Lessons—Notes on the Art of Surgery* (Chatto & Windus, 1981). In it he tells the following true story.

A surgeon stood by the bed of a young woman on whom he had just operated. Her mouth was paralysed and twisted—clownish. A tiny twig of her facial nerve, the one to the muscles of her mouth, had been severed. To remove the tumour in her cheek, the surgeon had had to sever the nerve.

'Will my mouth always be like this?' she asked. 'Yes,' said the surgeon, 'it will. It is because the nerve was cut.' She nodded and was silent. But her husband who was standing on the other side of the bed smiled.

'I like it,' he said. 'It's kind of cute.'

Then he bent down to kiss her crooked mouth. The surgeon watched, moved by the husband's love. As he kissed her, the husband twisted his own lips to accommodate hers, to show that his loving kiss still worked and that he still loved her.

I recently preached on one of the most famous passages in the Bible, 1 Corinthians 13, which defines love. At times like that, you feel like a pygmy facing Mount Everest. It's a tough sermon to preach but even tougher to live out, believe me.

I was reminded of the Japanese tourist in London seeking directions for Heathrow, as he was booked on a flight to Turkey. A well-meaning stranger put him on a train at Paddington, thinking he'd said that he wanted to get to Torquay! A lot of people reading 1 Corinthians 13 end up in Torquay instead of Turkey, figuratively speaking.

Because the passage deals with love, we wheel it out at weddings, funerals and speech days. It is such sublime prose that we treat it like Shakespeare and emboss it in frames and greeting cards. Because it is profound moral philosophy, we harness it in debates on ethics. But we are mistaken if we think it speaks of a love that we can attain alone.

Paul is writing of God's *agape* love, not based on emotion or attraction, but rather a decision of the will. God chooses to love things that are unlovely.

His love stoops to kiss that which has become deformed and, by that very act, to make it beautiful. No wonder it's called amazing grace.

For further reading

LUKE 6:27–36

We are not asked to manufacture *feelings* of love but to do *acts* of love, and Jesus points out here that the real test of love is when we exercise it towards those who hate us and harm us. We are called to be different from 'sinners' and to demonstrate this difference by loving those who are difficult to love as well as those we love naturally. Jesus wants us to treat our enemies in the opposite way to the way they treat us. We are not to avoid those who hate us but to 'do good' to them; we are to return blessings for curses. We are to do the unexpected, making ourselves vulnerable. When someone makes unreasonable demands on us, we are to offer even more than is asked. We are to lend to those whom we know will take advantage of us, knowing that we are unlikely to receive anything back. And when we do this, when we offer love with no strings attached, expecting nothing good in return, then God will reward us, for then we are most like him.

Prayer

Thank you, dear Lord, that you chose to love the unlovely, and that includes me. Teach me to do the same.

Joy

The joy of the Lord is your strength.
NEHEMIAH 8:10

In the unlikely event that I am approached by *Who's Who?* I have decided what to list under my special interests. Without doubt, one of my hobbies is people-watching. People are fascinating. I could watch them for hours, and summer holidays offer more time to indulge in my pastime. On a beach, a train or in a restaurant, there are plenty of opportunities to study human nature in all its wrinkled forms.

Standing in the arrivals hall at Gatwick the other morning, I was beating the boredom of waiting by studying my fellow travellers. Psychologists constantly seeking innovative personality tests could try a new one—the luggage carousel.

You can spot the anxious type—nervously biting the lip, scanning every passing suitcase with an expression of doom and gloom hanging over their heads like a rain cloud on Bank Holiday Monday. Then there's the suave, sophisticated, leather-luggage-with-embossed-initials type, looking suitably laid back, with sun tan to match. I even spotted a real-life power ranger in a slick business suit, barking into his mobile phone about how many minutes it would take before he 'hit' the office. I was treated to a fascinating survey of every personality type imaginable, and all for free.

Then I remembered (uncomfortably) something Jesus said about not judging people and not making quick assessments by what you see on the outside.

I recalled a man who regularly attended the church where I was a young, inexperienced minister. He always had a miserable look on his face, and often during a service I would catch a glimpse of his stony stare. Over the months I built a profile of him in my mind, neatly working out why he looked so depressed. Obviously, here was a staunch traditionalist who couldn't stand modern hymns, young people who made a noise and inexperienced ministers. Then one day, in a chance conversation, he told me of his excruciating arthritis that made sitting in church a real ordeal. But his love for his Lord meant that, no matter how uncomfortable he felt, being with God's people in worship was a highlight of his life.

As fascinating as people-watching can be, it's worth remembering that we only see through one pair of eyes, which have far from 20/20 vision.

For further reading

2 SAMUEL 6:12–23

Joy comes out of focusing on God rather than on ourselves and our circumstances, and it gives us the strength to do things that don't come easily. For the man described above, the joy he found in worshipping God with others in church enabled him to bear physical pain. King David totally forgot himself as he gave himself up to exuberant worship, while the ark was being brought into Jerusalem. But his wife, Michal, did not join in the rejoicing. As she watched from a window, she decided that David was being undignified in front of 'the slave girls of his servants' and when he went home to 'bless his household', instead of a joyful welcome he was met with a torrent of criticism (v. 20). If our expressions of joy make us look undignified to those around us, or if we don't look joyful in the way others think we should, we should not let that discourage us because God sees our hearts and delights in receiving our worship.

Prayer

Shout with joy to God, all the earth! Sing the glory of his name; make his praise glorious! (Psalm 66:1–2)

Peace

Peace I leave with you; my peace I give you.

JOHN 14:27

A visitor to an art gallery found that two exhibits shared the same title. The paintings were entitled 'Peace' but were totally different. The first was a rural landscape in which the artist had captured a perfect summer's day. The picture oozed tranquillity and invitingly beckoned the viewer to feel the warm sun and hear the gentle sounds of nature.

The second was a seascape with dark clouds and lashing rain. The picture showed a cliff-face standing proud against an angry sea. Everywhere was violent movement but in the cleft of the rock the artist had painted a bird on its nest. In the middle of a raging storm, the bird was resting in complete safety.

Those two interpretations of peace offer us a parable in troubled times. For some, peace is like a tranquil summer's day when nothing appears to disturb the picture. It is all about cloudless skies and endless sunshine. Thank God, such times do come.

But in reality, life is not always like that. Whichever scale we use to measure—global or personal, macro or micro—life produces storms from time to time. Interestingly, the second picture, of the bird resting in the middle of a howling gale, is closer to the Bible's teaching about God's gift of peace. Peace is not so much the absence of trouble but the relaxation of heart and mind that comes in the midst of trouble.

Paul was an influential church leader who wrote much of the New Testament. He saw peace as an important ingredient of the Christian message. He stressed the primary importance of individuals discovering peace with God. And that is only possible through all that Jesus achieved by dying and rising again.

Paul taught that peace *with* God is a gift that all can enjoy because of

Jesus. On the basis of this new relationship we can experience the peace *of* God in every circumstance that life throws up. He describes it as 'the peace of God which transcends all understanding' and speaks of the way it can 'guard your hearts and your minds' (Philippians 4:7).

As one writer of a previous generation expressed it, 'If God be our God, he will give us peace in trouble. When there is a storm without, he will make peace within. The world can create trouble in peace, but God can create peace in trouble.'

For further reading

JOHN 14:15–27

When Jesus speaks these words, he knows that he is about to be arrested and crucified. He is telling the disciples what they are unable to comprehend at this time, that although he is leaving them, the Holy Spirit will come to teach them and remind them of all he has said. Meanwhile, as they face turbulent times he leaves them his peace—and his peace is unique. The world gives a counterfeit peace that depends on nothing changing, on having money in the bank, a secure job, our own home, people we can depend on, good health, and all the things that cushion us against uncertainty and insecurity. The peace the world gives is dependent on things we cannot control. The peace God gives is dependent on him and he is totally dependable. God knows everything that will happen, and he is in everything that is happening. He does not leave us alone to bear our troubles; nor does he leave us unprovided for. As Paul discovered, God's 'grace is sufficient' for all our needs (2 Corinthians 12:9).

Prayer

In an uncertain world, Lord Jesus, thank you for the peace that you alone can give to me, that will never let me down.

Patience

Be still before the Lord and wait patiently for him; do not fret when men succeed in their ways, when they carry out their wicked schemes.

PSALM 37:7

I once visited Belfast, after a group of churches had invited me to speak at a series of public meetings. On the Saturday afternoon, I visited the so-called 'Peace Line' which separates Loyalist and Republican areas.

The Peace Line is a thick wall about twelve feet high that creates a physical barrier between housing areas notorious for disturbances. Access from one side to the other is via roads sheltered by steel gates and guard posts. When all is calm, the gates are open—but they can be shut and manned by police or soldiers at the first sign of trouble.

The wall dividing Berlin came down some years ago, but the wall in Belfast stays standing.

I have been a frequent visitor to Northern Ireland through much of what we call 'the Troubles'. I have observed rollercoaster emotions as the political situation has followed its topsy-turvy course. On this occasion, as the latest talks at Stormont dragged on, I went to the wall to offer yet another prayer for peace. I came away feeling bleak and empty.

A couple of hours later, I met a man who changed my view. He had come to hear me speak and we were introduced at the end of the meeting. He told me his story.

Brought up in a staunchly Loyalist area, he was recruited by the paramilitaries at the tender age of twelve. He spent his teenage years in terrorist activities of the worst kind. On his eighteenth birthday he was convicted and sentenced to prison and there he stayed for thirteen and a half years. During the final years of his sentence he underwent a profound spiritual experience and left jail a committed follower of Jesus.

Since then he has become a community worker in one of the roughest housing estates in Belfast and now spends his time building relationships with young people on both sides of the sectarian divide, persuading them that the road to peace lies in a different direction from the one he once took.

As I listened to this man, I saw the sun of hope breaking through dark clouds of despair.

The Bible says of Jesus, 'He himself is our peace, who has made the two one and has destroyed the barrier, the dividing wall of hostility' (Ephesians 2:14). Only a change of heart can lead to a change of behaviour.

On that Saturday night, thank God, I spotted a crack in the wall.

For further reading

PSALM 40:1–17

Over many years people have worked and prayed for peace in Northern Ireland, often to see renewed hopes dashed by some new atrocity or setback. Humanly speaking, it would be easier to give up, to accept that things may never change and make the best of the way things are. The patience that comes from God is not like that. It is a patience that is prepared to wait and work for as long as it takes, believing that God is working behind the scenes and that he will bring good out of evil, however dark things look now. It is not about a grim endurance but about going on hoping even when there seem no grounds for hope. It is a patience that overcomes discouragement and opposition. We may be called to exercise patience in our work in the world or in something closer to home and much more personal. God's Holy Spirit will help us in this, and every so often he will show us reasons for going on waiting patiently for God to act.

Prayer

Help me, Heavenly Father, to 'be joyful in hope, patient in affliction, faithful in prayer' (Romans 12:12).

Kindness

Blessed is he who is kind to the needy.
PROVERBS 14:21

In 1975 a little boy named Raymond Dunn was born in the USA. Complications surrounding his birth led to a skull fracture and oxygen deprivation. Raymond was severely retarded and, as the months went by, other problems appeared. His twisted body suffered up to 20 seizures a day and he was blind, mute and immobile. He had certain allergies that limited him to only one type of food—a meat-based formula produced by Gerber Foods.

In 1985 Gerber stopped making the formula that Raymond lived on. His mother embarked on a search across America, buying up old stocks of the food wherever she could. She accumulated cases of the product but, in spite of her efforts, by 1990 supplies ran out.

In desperation, Carol Dunn appealed to Gerber Foods for help. This was the only food her son could cope with; without it he could starve to death.

The employees of Gerber were told of the situation. In an unprecedented response they volunteered to work without pay to bring out old equipment, set up a production line and secure government approval for the food formula to be produced once more—all for one special customer.

In January 1995, Raymond Dunn died. He had become known as 'the Gerber boy' through press reports of the wonderful, compassionate response his need had evoked in people who had never met him.

Such heart-warming stories stir the emotions and make you proud to be human.

But why, I found myself asking as I read that report, are we held in such a straitjacket of impotence with the humanity and injustice that, in Bosnia, lies on our own European doorstep?

Surely if the plight of one helpless young man could prompt such a practical response from complete strangers, couldn't we have done more to help the suffering people of Sarajevo, Bihac, Tuzla and Gorazde?

I thank God for those who are there to offer help as relief workers and peacekeepers, but despite the brave efforts, the tragedy continues, proving the sad truth of Neville Chamberlain's words: 'In war, whichever side may call itself the victor, there are no winners, but all are losers.'

Pray God that someone, somewhere, somehow will break this deadly stranglehold.

But as with the plight of Raymond Dunn, it will take imagination, a large measure of selflessness and, above all else, compassion.

For further reading

John 6:1–13

All four Gospels tell the story of the feeding of the five thousand, but only John mentions that the meagre amount of food from which Jesus fed the multitude was provided by a boy in the crowd. We don't even know his name, and the other Gospel writers didn't think him worth mentioning. Instead of satisfying his own hunger, he willingly offered his 'five small barley loaves and two small fish' to the disciples to share (v. 9). He looked beyond himself to the needs of others. Perhaps something Jesus had said had so impressed him that this was his response. Kindness is measured not by how much we are able to give but by how willing we are. For the Gerber employees, their great effort benefited only one person, but they still felt it was worth doing. And this story shows that even the smallest gift can be multiplied by God to bless many.

Prayer

Thank you, Lord, for the examples of kindness set me by the Gerber employees and the seemingly insignificant boy in Jesus' time. Help me to see the opportunities you give me to be kind to others.

Goodness

No good tree bears bad fruit, nor does a bad tree bear good fruit.
LUKE 6:43

Honesty pays—or does it? London Transport thinks so, and is well into a major drive to stamp out Tube fare dodgers. On-the-spot fines for travelling without a valid ticket have been introduced, backed up by a large advertising campaign.

The ads extol the virtues of being honest, pointing out that the expense and embarrassment caused when you're caught fare-dodging are not worth the hassle.

My favourite shows an elderly lady telling how she was driving her Morris Minor in London when she was flagged down by an anxious pedestrian. He told her he was the lead singer with the rock band U2 who were playing a concert at Wembley Stadium. His transport had not turned up and the concert couldn't start without him. Could she possibly help by giving him a lift?

You can picture the scene. A touching rebuke to the so-called generation gap is administered by an elderly soul prepared to put herself out for a young stranger. She skilfully negotiates her way through the rush-hour traffic, carrying our hero to his adoring, waiting fans.

So, the following day she is relating this touching story to the world. 'What did the rock star look like?' she is asked.

Her reply leaves everyone speechless: 'He was in his mid-sixties, bald, overweight, wearing a red and white scarf and a rosette bearing the message, "Arsenal for the cup"'!

The point of the ad, it seems, is that it is easier to pay your fare than to make up elaborate excuses as to why you haven't bought a ticket.

But how honest is honest? We may applaud a scheme to deter fare dodgers or set up a Neighbourhood Watch. But what about the provocative question posed by this title of a book that recently landed on my desk: *Who Are You When Nobody Is Looking?*

I recently read a news report about a taxi driver in Beijing who found the equivalent of £19,000 in cash left by a very careless passenger.

The man handed it in, despite the fact that it represented a lifetime's salary for a taxi driver in that country. We don't know what motivated him, but what he did was probably the most difficult act of his life. But I'm sure he feels a better man for his decision.

Human experience bears out that deceit, lies and cover-ups may bring short-term relief but end in long-term disaster. Honesty really does pay.

For further reading

PSALM 15:1–5; LUKE 6:43–45

We might use many different words, including 'honesty', to describe goodness. We might say that one outstanding act proves that a person must be good, as in the story of the taxi driver, because a bad person would not have behaved in that way. In Luke 6, Jesus says that the way we behave will be consistent with whether we are good or bad, because we are motivated by what is in our hearts. If the Holy Spirit is developing goodness in us, it will show up in every area of our life. Psalm 15 describes a person who displays his goodness in how he lives, the things he says, and how he handles money. For him, doing what is right is not one consideration of several but the only consideration, 'even when it hurts'. At the end of the psalm we are told, 'He who does these things will never be shaken' (v. 5). If we live good lives, we will know security and stability, whatever choices and temptations we may face.

Prayer

'Create in me a pure heart, O God, and renew a steadfast spirit within me'
(Psalm 51:10).

Faithfulness

I have set the Lord always before me. Because he is at my right hand, I shall not be shaken.

PSALM 16:8

What's the best thing to do when you are faced with something that scares you half to death? Some of us find it easier to run away, while others stand their ground and confront whatever frightens them. Fight or flight—which to choose?

Our living nightmares come in different guises. Yours may be standing up to make a presentation in front of several hundred people; your neighbour may fear a sudden ring of the telephone, heralding bad news; mine could be a painful confrontation with someone I would rather avoid.

Most of us are familiar with that sick, gnawing feeling at the centre of our stomach, reminding us that what we dread is about to happen.

Someone once asked me if I thought Jesus could have avoided going to the cross. I am convinced that he could. How else do we make sense of his heartfelt prayer a few hours before the crucifixion: 'Father, if you are willing, take this cup from me; yet not my will, but yours be done' (Luke 22:42)?

Jesus willingly accepted the will of God, recognizing that a greater purpose was being worked out that went beyond his own immediate well-being.

Most of us find this the biggest fear of all—that God's will for my life may involve pain, separation and sacrifice.

But Jesus was driven by a deeper motivation. The Bible explains it this way: 'for the joy set before him [he] endured the cross' (Hebrews 12:2).

Beyond Good Friday Jesus could see Easter Sunday; after the cross there was an empty grave. Jesus looked beyond the immediate to the ultimate.

G.K. Chesterton tells the story of Francis of Assisi, who was terrified of leprosy. One day he met a leper walking down a country road. Instinctively he recoiled from the sight of such a horribly deformed person. Feeling ashamed of such a violent reaction, Francis steeled himself and approached the leper. He put his arms around the man's neck and embraced him. He continued on his journey and, after a few paces, turned to look again at the leper. The open road was empty. From that moment on, Francis lived with the belief that he had not met a leper that day, but Christ himself.

By facing what we fear, we can find resurrection, and that is true not only at Easter, but during every week of the year.

For further reading

DANIEL 6:1–23

Daniel was a man of integrity in every area of his life, serving his earthly king as faithfully as he did his heavenly King. He was 'trustworthy, and neither corrupt nor negligent' (v. 4) and was rewarded with promotions. His devotion to God was something he did not hide and his enemies saw this as a means to get rid of him (v. 5). Daniel's practice was to pray three times a day by his window. When Darius' thoughtless edict was issued, it would have been understandable if Daniel had decided to give up praying for thirty days, or at least to have concealed what he was doing. However, he had made up his mind to be faithful to God and he did not alter his practice in any way. And when he prayed, he not only asked for help but gave thanks to God (vv. 10–11). God rewarded his faithfulness and trust and saved him, against the odds. If faithfulness is our habit when life is easy, then although we may struggle when the hard times come, we are much less likely to fall away

Prayer

Faithful God, you never let me down. Your love for me will never fail because it depends on your faithfulness and not on mine. I depend on you for all that this life may hold and for eternity.

Gentleness

Written 27 January 2001

**Do nothing out of selfish ambition or vain conceit, but in humility
consider others better than yourselves.**
PHILIPPIANS 2:3

The name Govind Bawji is not one that trips lightly off the tongue and
until recently I'd never heard of the gentleman.

He died last week in India after fifty years' service as a baggage man
to a succession of touring cricket teams. To call him a baggage man is not
fair, as he went to great lengths to provide for the comfort and security
of players under his care. His greatest honour was to look after the MCC
on their tours of the sub-continent and he became a legendary figure,
serving eight England managers and captains.

His job was to ensure that the team luggage arrived safely and that the
needs of the tourers were met, which sometimes led him to sleep across
the doorways of captains' rooms when he felt their security might be
threatened. His proud claim was that he never lost a bag in thousands
of miles of travel.

Former England captain David Gower summed up Govind Bawji's
loyal service: 'If anyone needed anything mended—a pad strap or something like that—he'd either do it or get it done. Nothing was too much
trouble. He was impeccable.'

That's quite a tribute to someone who never played in a Test Match,
yet in his own way contributed to their success.

I have met people like Govind Bawji—people who see serving others
not as an imposition but a privilege and who don't regard the concept of
service as demeaning, but rather a calling. Such people are a rare find.

The image of a servant is widely used in the New Testament to describe what a follower of Christ should look and act like. Strictly speaking, the word often used does not mean 'servant' so much as 'slave'. It means one who is so totally owned by another that his will is consumed by their wishes and needs.

Jesus spoke of the servant principle often, not least with regard to the way we treat others: 'Whoever wants to become great among you must be your servant' (Matthew 20:26). I was reminded of that statement when I read of Govind's quiet efficiency. Nothing was too much trouble for someone who took his responsibilities seriously.

The testimonials to an Indian gentleman I'd never met gave this rather inadequate and part-time follower of Christ a timely prod. Servanthood, you see, is about how you live and what you give.

For further reading

1 THESSALONIANS 2:6–12; PROVERBS 15:1; 25:15

It is very hard to define gentleness, but it is a trait that is unmistakable in people who have forgotten themselves in serving others. They are willing to humble themselves; they show consideration for others, sometimes at the cost of their own 'rights'; and they don't demand recognition or gratitude for what they do. When Paul talks of his service to the church in Thessalonica, he compares it to the gentleness of 'a mother caring for her little children' (v. 7) and of a father 'encouraging, comforting and urging' the believers 'to live lives worthy of God' (vv. 11–12). Paul and his friends were 'delighted' to share everything with the Thessalonian church despite the 'toil and hardship' this cost them (vv. 8–9). They did not threaten or bully but gently led by example and service. It would be easy to mistake gentleness for weakness, but lest we should, the verses in Proverbs remind us of the surprisingly powerful effect of a gentle answer to defuse anger, and of a gentle word to influence the powerful.

Prayer

Father God, help me to show your gentleness in the way that I speak and behave to those around me.

Self-control

In your anger do not sin.

PSALM 4:4

Have you heard the one about the cannibal who arrived home from his holiday minus a leg? When asked what had happened, he replied that self-catering has its drawbacks.

I was reminded of that story when reading of outbreaks of 'road rage' during these recent hot summer weeks. In one case a motorist fired several shots from a revolver after an incident with another driver, all in broad daylight in a South London street.

In another report, a woman battered her Toyota with a golf club after it broke down. In shades of Basil Fawlty, the lady set about smashing lights and windscreen, blaming it all on a depressing round of golf.

Why do tempers flare when temperatures soar? Is there a connection between the heat outside and inside?

Road rage is a comparatively new thing. Motorists have probably shouted at each other since the days of the Model T Ford, but the disturbing modern trend of violent words turning to violent actions gives cause for concern.

It highlights the need for self-control at all levels of society, not simply on the road. From the football terraces to the saloon bar, from the classroom to the boardroom, from playgroup to Parliament, we could all do with some help in handling hassle well. I am not talking about creating a race of humanoids with sickly grins, who simply chant, 'Have a nice day!' to all and sundry. It's about learning to express our feelings and frustrations without crossing the boundaries of acceptable behaviour. I am intrigued by the verse in the Bible which says, 'In your anger do not sin.' It tells me that it is possible to be angry but without breaking God's law.

It was G.K. Chesterton who said, 'People generally quarrel because they cannot argue.' When we feed our need for excessive anger, we do so at great cost to ourselves and those around us. Like the cannibal, we end up the loser.

Perhaps a crash course for motorists (forgive the pun) would show us how to let off steam without letting ourselves down.

For further reading

1 SAMUEL 24:1–22

David had cause to be angry with Saul. He was on the run and in fear of losing his life because of Saul's unfounded suspicions against him and others had been murdered because of the help they had given him (1 Samuel 22:1–22). When Saul came into the cave alone, it must have looked like a God-given opportunity to David (it certainly did to his men) to solve his problems, to avenge the deaths of others and to achieve God's purpose of making him king of Israel. But David acted with great self-control, merely cutting off a piece of Saul's robe—and even that he bitterly regretted (v. 5). David was able to control himself because he knew that God was in ultimate control and he had put his trust in him. He left it with God to act (v. 12) and refused to take matters into his own hands. However unfairly he may have felt he had been treated, in his anger he refused to sin and so should we.

Prayer

Remind me, Lord, to think before I act. Teach me to be self-controlled, especially in the unexpected and unwelcome things that I have to face.

Doorways to Forgiveness

First things first

We all, like sheep, have gone astray, each of us has turned to his own way; and the Lord has laid on him the iniquity of us all.
ISAIAH 53:6

Question: How many men does it take to change an empty toilet roll?
Answer: No one knows as it's never been attempted.

Now, although I don't personally subscribe to such a sexist view, I will admit to one thing. I have no interest in what makes things work—I just want them to work. Now, please.

One example is the super-swift laptop that I am using to type these words. A colleague who advised me on its purchase is a total anorak on such matters. For months he has bombarded me with facts, figures and technobabble way beyond my limited understanding.

When my new machine arrived, he treated me to a full-blown induction session in which my gigabytes and docking station were thoroughly explored and explained. After an hour he paused for breath and asked if I had any questions. I did—but wished I didn't. 'Can you go through how to switch it on again?' I asked hesitantly. His look said it all.

Earlier this week I had another technical encounter of an uncomfortable kind, this time with a nice lady from the mobile phone company. All morning I had been trying to make a call only to discover that there was no signal. In frustration I rang the company. Was there a problem with my account? Were they experiencing difficulties with the network? Was the local transmitter down?

The lady asked me to take the back off the phone and remove the tiny SIM card. Could I see a little gold strip? Then could I rub it carefully with a clean cloth and replace it? Oh dear, a perfect signal in seconds. Confused and embarrassed, I apologized for wasting her time. 'No

problem, sir,' she purred. 'We get a lot of... er, people like you who...'
I cut her off before she could finish. I already felt enough like Victor
Meldrew.

I remember a man I once met. Everything around him was wrong—
his wife, his job, his friends. Not one of them matched his expectations.
But the thought had never occurred to him that he was looking at the
world with less than perfect vision. Change was needed first within
himself. And that surely is the toughest, yet most important, change
of all.

For further reading

ROMANS 7:14–25; ACTS 3:19–20

Are there situations in your life where you start out with good intentions
but then, when it comes to the crunch, you let yourself down? Life can
become an endless cycle of deciding to do better, failing and then resolving to do better next time. Perhaps we identify with Paul's frustration
when he says, 'For what I do is not the good I want to do; no, the evil
I do not want to do—this I keep on doing' (Romans 7:19). But there is
an answer: 'Thanks be to God—through Jesus Christ our Lord' (v. 25).
Peter says, 'Repent, then, and turn to God so that your sins may be
wiped out.' We need to change direction from living life our own way to
living it God's way, acknowledging our inability to live a 'good enough'
life without his help and believing that because Jesus has borne the
punishment for our wrongdoing by dying on the cross, we will be
acceptable to him. A computer needs to be switched on before it is of
any use. We need to be rescued from our sin and failure (v. 24) before
we can begin to live to the full the life we were created for.

Prayer

*Lord Jesus, thank you for dying on the cross in order that I can be made
clean and set free from sin.*

Who's to blame?

Why do you look at the speck of sawdust in your brother's eye and pay no attention to the plank in your own eye?
MATTHEW 7:3

A man was concerned that his wife's hearing was getting worse, and decided to test it out. Standing in the kitchen, he called his wife who was in the sitting-room. No reply came, so he moved into the hallway and called her name again. Still no reply. Now almost convinced his theory was correct, he quietly slipped into the room, stood behind the chair, still out of her line of vision, and again called her. With a disgruntled sigh she looked up from her knitting and said, 'For the third time, what do you want?'

Why is it, we always assume that someone else is to blame? If things go wrong, it is almost an automatic response to look around for a likely candidate to point the finger at. It is a weakness we all suffer from to one degree or another.

Jesus Christ, in his famous Sermon on the Mount, painted an almost ludicrous picture when he asked the question, 'Why do you look at the speck of sawdust in your brother's eye and pay no attention to the plank in your own eye?' He was warning against the hypocrisy of passing judgment on others carelessly when there are greater faults in our own lives.

We could all do with less haste and more circumspection when it comes to assessing others, as this anonymous 'short course on effective leadership in management' suggests:

The six most important words:
    I admit I made a mistake.

The five most important words:
I am proud of you.

The four most important words:
What is your opinion?

The three most important words:
If you please.

The two most important words:
Thank you.

The one most important word:
We.

The least important word:
I.

For further reading

GENESIS 3:1–19

Being able to say, 'It was my fault; I was to blame' is something we all need to learn because it doesn't come naturally. Blaming someone else for what I did wrong has a long history, going all the way back to Adam and Eve in the garden of Eden. Acknowledging, if only to themselves, that they had disobeyed God, they hid from him. For the first time they felt naked, ashamed and vulnerable. Then, when God questioned them about their disobedience, Adam blamed Eve and Eve blamed the serpent! Knowing that we are in the wrong is a horrible feeling, whether other people know about it or only God. But unlike Adam and Eve, we do not have to go on feeling ashamed and guilty. Jesus has paid the price for our wrongdoing; forgiveness and a fresh start are freely available to us. All we have to do is receive them.

Prayer

'Therefore there is now no condemnation for those who are in Christ Jesus, because through Christ Jesus the law of the Spirit of life set me free from the law of sin and death' (Romans 8:1–2). Praise God!

Putting things right

Therefore he is able to save completely those who come to God
through him, because he always lives to intercede for them.

HEBREWS 7:25

How about some good news for a change? James and Sue Marshall live in
Manchester. In 1991 their home was burgled, but they got off lightly as
the thief grabbed the first thing that came to hand, a personal stereo.

The incident was almost forgotten until a few weeks ago. James was
fixing his car when a man approached the house carrying a parcel.
Opening it, the astonished couple found a brand new personal stereo,
twenty pounds in cash and a note from the man who had burgled their
home.

The note explained that he wanted to compensate the family for his
dishonesty. He had now found God, and the Lord had forgiven him. In
making a new start he wanted to put matters right. Sue Marshall
commented, 'We couldn't believe it after all this time. We don't know
who the thief is but we want him to know that we do forgive him.' A
rather bemused police spokesman said, 'It would be nice if a few more
thieves round here had similar pangs of conscience.'

That press report reminded me of two statements, one by Jesus
and the other by a policeman. Take the long arm of the law first. I was
discussing a serious case with the detective in charge and pointed out
that the defendant appeared to be sorry for what he'd done. I've never
forgotten the oficer's reply: 'I've been in this job many years. When most
people say, "I'm sorry", they generally mean, "I'm sorry I got caught."
Very few mean, "I'm sorry I ever did it."'

As for Jesus, the incident that sprang to mind was a meeting with
Zacchaeus, a man with a dubious moral track record. He was a public
official who spent most of his career ripping people off and making a

fortune into the bargain. Meeting Jesus, he decided it was time to change and promptly announced that 50 per cent of his earnings were to be given to the poor, and those he had swindled would receive four times what had been taken. All of this prompted Jesus to say, 'Today salvation has come to this house, because this man, too, is a son of Abraham. For the Son of Man came to seek and to save what was lost' (Luke 19:9–10).

From Jericho to Manchester, it's good to know that the lost-and-found business is still booming.

For further reading

LUKE 23:33–34; HEBREWS 7:23–28

Jesus did not say to those who were crucifying him, 'I forgive you' but 'Father, forgive them…' (Luke 23:34). In this prayer he was showing his tormentors who he was and who his Father was, for only God can forgive sins (Mark 2:7). As the agony of his death began, he was praying for the very forgiveness that it would make possible. His prayer anticipated his work in heaven where, as he lives before God the Father with the visible marks of his crucifixion, he intercedes for us (Hebrews 7:25). This prayer in the Gospel of Luke also teaches us about how we should forgive those who wrong us. We are to forgive them unconditionally, not wanting God to hold their fault against them. Forgiveness is rarely easy and we may be tempted to pray, 'Father, you forgive them because I can't', but God will give us the ability to forgive if we ask him, especially as we remember how he has forgiven us at such a high price.

Prayer

If you need to, pray the following prayer:

I am finding it very hard to forgive…………. Lord, you know how much they have hurt me, but because you have forgiven me and I want to please you, give me the ability to let go of my hurt and anger and truly forgive them.

Making the first move

Written in May 1996.

How good and pleasant it is when brothers live together in unity.
PSALM 133:1

The two men were brothers but their relationship was strained. Eventually, one, totally consumed by jealousy, murdered the other. Some would say religion caused it, but such a superficial diagnosis misses the heart of the problem. It was smouldering resentment, fuelled by the impulse of an angry moment—and a man lay dead.

God had seen it coming and issued the jealous brother a stark choice in letters ten feet high: 'Why are you angry? Why is your face downcast? If you do what is right, will you not be accepted? But if you do not do what is right, sin is crouching at your door; it desires to have you, but you must master it' (Genesis 4:6–7). The advice was rejected and the first murder in history was committed by Cain. The innocent victim was his brother, Abel.

Last Sunday lunch-time, another murder took place. On the slip road of the M25, 21-year-old Stephen Cameron stepped out of his car to remonstrate with an aggressive motorist. Within seconds he lay dying from stab wounds. All week we have heard opinions about this bizarre phenomenon of the 1990s—road rage. The phrase, first coined in the USA, defines an uncontrollable anger that seizes people who get behind the wheel of a vehicle, causing them to explode with furious words, gestures and physical violence.

We are told that it is a reflection of our competitive society. Deadlines to meet, traffic to beat, seem to turn up the heat on our simmering emotions. Some say it's Stone Age aggression in 20th-century clothes. We see both car and road as our territory, to be defended at all costs against those with the temerity to invade our private space.

But as many know to their cost, such rage is not confined to roads. You find it in the office, playground or kitchen. The important thing to notice from God's warning to Cain is that none of us can claim to be helpless victims of our emotions. There's no room for the 'my father made me like this' type of excuse that we clutch like a moral fig leaf to hide our embarrassment. Sin lies close at everyone's elbow and the secret of mastering it lies in an act of the will. And, as always, God never asks us to do something that he is not prepared to help us with.

Heaven's grace remains the best fire extinguisher.

For further reading

GENESIS 27:41–45; 32:6–8; 33:1–10

There are several stories in the Bible about the strained relationships between brothers—Cain and Abel, David's sons, and Joseph and his brothers, to mention a few. The story of Jacob and Esau is an encouraging one. Jacob had cheated Esau out of his father's blessing and had then run away to escape Esau's murderous wrath. He returned home many years later in fear and trepidation. He was not reassured to hear that Esau was coming to meet him, accompanied by 400 men! But the story has a happy ending. God had blessed Esau and he was no longer angry. He was coming to welcome Jacob and his family, and Jacob was overwhelmed: 'For to see your face is like seeing the face of God, now that you have received me favourably' (33:10). Time moves on and people don't stay the same. Is there someone in your family with whom you need to be reconciled? Is God saying to you that it's time for you to make the first move towards restoring the relationship? Perhaps you will find in doing so that the person from whom you have been estranged was just hoping that you would approach them.

Prayer

Teach me to forgive, for my heart is stony,
Help me to reflect the love which has reclaimed me.
Father, when my pride burns, make me humble like a child,
Each day may our hearts through Jesus Christ be reconciled.

STUART SINCLAIR (REPRINTED BY PERMISSION)

Happy families

One of Tony Blair's children hit the headlines in July 2000.
This 'open letter' was written by Ian Coffey a few days later.

His father saw him and was filled with compassion for him.
LUKE 15:20

Dear Tony Blair,

I appreciated the honesty of your statement on Thursday that it is sometimes easier to be Prime Minister than to be a parent.

The last thing your family needs today is well-meaning advice. From the outside it looks as if you are a happy, balanced bunch who could probably teach the rest of us a thing or two.

The purpose of this letter is to say I feel for you and would encourage you to hang in there for the sake of your own kids and fellow members of the Struggling-Hard-To-Be-Good-Parents-Club.

All teenagers make mistakes. Come to think of it, all human beings make mistakes. But it's a double whammy to blow it at sixteen and then find you are the lead story in the news.

One of my sons had a similar experience as a young teenager and decided with a bunch of friends to experiment with alcohol. We were at a Christian conference at the time where my wife and I were taking seminars on family and marriage. Our son drank so much vodka, he collapsed in a toilet cubicle and was carried back to our room unconscious. We spent an anxious night by his bedside.

In the cold light of day we talked and a very sober and sore-headed young man explained what had happened. Because his youth group had a strict 'no alcohol' rule, he was sent home from the event and banned from attending anything similar for a time. Disgrace with a big 'D'.

It was a difficult time for him and for us all as a family. When you are a minister you live in a goldfish bowl. When you are Prime Minister you live in a bigger version of the same thing. People have their opinions. The nice ones keep them to themselves.

We are a few years on from that uncomfortable period. The son in question is now a level-headed young man we are extremely proud of. He is warm, sociable, witty and bright. Most of his friends would describe him as someone good to have around in a crisis. I'd trust him with my life. And one day he will make a great father.

Oh yes, he has a healthy caution as far as alcohol is concerned. So hard-won lessons can be valuable in the long run.

With best wishes,
Ian Coffey

For further reading

LUKE 15:11–31

Being a parent is a learning experience. One of the hardest lessons to learn is letting go and allowing our children independence and the freedom to make choices, some of which we may not agree with. Perhaps some of Jesus' parables were 'based on a true story'. Certainly the relationships within this particular parable sound authentic: the rebellious son, jealous brother, loving father. Letting his younger son go was costly to his father in more than financial terms; he would have worried about him and missed him. Perhaps he often looked into the distance, hoping to see him return (v. 20). When the son did come back, obviously poorer than when he had left, there were no questions, no recriminations, but a warm welcome and an extravagant party to celebrate. It is noteworthy that the son felt able to come home, even though he did not expect to be received on the same terms as before. When we let our children go, we should make sure that they know we will always love them, whatever they do, just as God loves us.

Prayer

Heavenly Father, I know that Jesus told this parable to show that repentant sinners are welcomed by you. Thank you that you have shown that to be true in my case.

Doorways to Encouraging Others

The burden of leadership

'I cannot carry all these people by myself; the burden is too heavy for me.'
NUMBERS 11:14

Having spent the last couple of weeks in Australia, I arrived at Heathrow yesterday morning feeling more than a little tired. Brushing aside the after-effects of a long, crowded flight and the soggy, cold welcome of a wet London morning, I sought some comfort in a newspaper.

I caught a headline: 'Love thyself, clergy commanded.' I did a double-take to make sure that jet-lag was not playing tricks with my eyes. It was a serious report on a conference held this week for clergymen feeling the pressure of running a local church. One of the organizers commented, 'Clergy have been very good at taking care of others but not so good at looking after themselves.'

The conference came up with a list of 'Ten Commandments' to help ease the pressures:

* Thou shalt not try to be all things to all people.
* Thou shalt not be perfect or even try.
* Thou shalt leave undone things that ought not to be done.
* Thou shalt not spread thyself too thin.
* Thou shalt learn to say 'no'.
* Thou shalt schedule time for thyself and thy supportive network.
* Thou shalt switch off and do nothing regularly.
* Thou shalt be boring, inelegant, untidy and unattractive at times.
* Thou shalt not feel guilty.
* Thou shalt not be thine own worst enemy.

Now for those who know little about the role, I guess there will be a few raised eyebrows at the very thought that being a vicar could be even remotely stressful. After all, if you only work one day in seven, and then only for a couple of hours. It's hardly the fast lane of the adrenaline highway, is it?

As a local businessman said to me recently on hearing of my job, 'I suppose you must spend a lot of time with elderly people then?'

The truth is, being a minister is what you make of it. It can be a very lazy life, but most of those I know see it not as a job but as a calling. They give of themselves freely with no interest in financial reward.

So maybe you know a minister somewhere who could do with a copy of these ten commandments and, even better still, a word of thanks and encouragement.

For further reading

EXODUS 18:7–27

Sometimes we are too close to a situation to see it objectively, and this can be true of those in leadership too. Moses' father-in-law, Jethro, came to visit and was able to look with fresh eyes at all that was going on. He quickly realized that Moses was in danger of wearing himself out and the people as well, as they queued up waiting for him to decide their disputes. He advised Moses to delegate some of the work to others. Moses followed Jethro's advice and his burden was considerably lessened. Perhaps you are in a position of leadership and God is telling you to relinquish some of your duties so that others may gain experience and you may have more time and energy available. On the other hand, perhaps you know a leader who is flagging and needs encouragement, support or some constructive advice. Could you be a Jethro to him or her?

Prayer

Pray for wisdom for those in positions of leadership to know how to manage their time, and what to say 'no' to. Ask God to show you how you can encourage and support them.

No kindness is too small

May the Lord show mercy to the household of Onesiphorus, because he often refreshed me and was not ashamed of my chains.
2 TIMOTHY 1:16

How about some good news to brighten up the day? Often we feel so swamped by problems belonging to others and ourselves that we find it almost impossible to believe that there is any good news around.

This morning I came across a story about a footballer. (Oh no, not another story about a footballer. The nation's soccer stars don't always have a good press, and the off-the-field antics of some have not offered a positive role model to their fans. But this time it's good news—honestly.)

Chris Powell plays for Charlton and England. One of his greatest fans has been a young man called Andrew Mills, who hardly missed a Charlton game. Andrew was disabled so sat in the same section of the ground each week.

It became a special arrangement at each match that Chris Powell looked out for Andrew and gave him a wave. Just before Christmas 2001, Andrew was taken seriously ill and admitted to hospital for treatment.

On Christmas Day at 8.30am a special visitor arrived on the ward unannounced. It was Chris Powell bearing a gift—an autographed England shirt. Sadly, Andrew died two days later, but a simple gesture of kindness and interest made a difference to a teenager's life, when so much was stacked against him.

Jesus taught a simple yet profound principle: 'So in everything, do to others what you would have them do to you, for this sums up the Law and the Prophets' (Matthew 7:12). This has been called the Golden Rule, as it offers a guiding light about the decisions and choices we face daily.

According to Jesus, it sums up the hundreds of pages of the Old Testament scriptures in a single memorable phrase—treat others how you want them to treat you. (I like the sharp proviso that someone once added: 'Do unto others, even when they never do unto you!')

William Wordsworth wrote:

> The best portion of a good man's life,
> His little, nameless, unremembered acts
> Of kindness and love.

It's uplifting to read good news, but better still to go out and make some of my own.

For further reading

2 TIMOTHY 1:8–18

Rejection hurts. The desertion of his friends when he was made a prisoner clearly hurt Paul. Perhaps he singled out Phygelus and Hermogenes by name (v. 15) because he had thought that they, at least, would have stood by him through thick and thin. The kindness of Onesiphorus shines even more brightly because he seems to have been the only one to remain loyal, going to the trouble of finding Paul and then ministering to his needs. Rejection hurts, but to be overlooked is painful too. Sometimes people in wheelchairs say that they get ignored as people literally overlook them, talking to the people with them but not to them. And they are not the only ones. For various reasons there are people who just don't seem to get noticed. They feel that they are not cared for or that they don't matter to anyone. Just to be acknowledged would mean so much. A small kindness from us would cost little but be so much appreciated.

Prayer

Heavenly Father, is there someone near me that I have not noticed, who feels lonely and overlooked? Show me how to build small kindnesses into my daily life, because I know how much I appreciate the kindness of others to me.

What did you say?

Let your conversation be always full of grace, seasoned with salt, so that you may know how to answer everyone.
COLOSSIANS 4:6

Can you look back at a significant moment in your life that, in some way, became a turning point?

According to Cherie Booth, the Prime Minister's wife, such a moment occurred in her childhood. She recently related how a teacher at school made a suggestion that changed the course of her life.

Following the break-up of her parents' marriage, her schoolwork was suffering. A far-sighted teacher suggested that Cherie should be put up a year at school, in the belief that the challenge would bring out the best in her. Cherie Booth maintains that the decision paid off, and attributes her formidable academic achievements to that recommendation.

If nothing else, this story reminds us of the critical role teachers play in the development of children, and at a time when the teaching profession is coming in for more than its fair share of criticism, I believe that it underlines their value and importance. Most of the teachers I know are hardworking, dedicated professionals doing their best to perform in a system that makes more demands while, at the same time, cutting back on resources.

The phrase 'a defining moment' seems fashionable at present, but it is true that there are pivotal people in each of our lives that set a course for our future. It may be a teacher, a friend, a parent or the boss at work. In the complex network of relationships that make up our lives, the chances are that most of us have the potential to influence someone else, either positively or negatively.

An incident occurred a couple of days ago when a close friend of mine had a brief conversation with someone going through a difficult time. My friend didn't have a clue about the problem but went out of his way to praise the person's work, commend them on their efficiency and thank them for their commitment.

The result of that chance encounter was that someone with low self-esteem suddenly felt appreciated. That is why the Bible constantly encourages us to be on the look-out for other people's interests. This applies to our words as well as actions. That is why we are told, 'Let your conversation be always full of grace, seasoned with salt, so that you may know how to answer everyone.'

Who knows? Something said today could prove to be a defining moment in someone else's life.

For further reading

JAMES 3:3–8; COLOSSIANS 4:2–6

James vividly illustrates how such a seemingly small thing as the tongue is able to inflict great damage. He talks about it being 'a world of evil' that 'corrupts the whole person… and is itself set on fire by hell' (v. 6). It is tempting to think that James is overstating the case, but therein lies the danger. How can we be more aware of the potential for harm in what we say and seek to avoid it? Paul puts the positive case for the tongue in Colossians. If we 'devote' ourselves to prayer, cultivating inner conversation with God at all times, being 'watchful and thankful', we will be much less inclined to stir up trouble with our words. It is impossible to be thankful and critical or malicious at the same time. Conversation that is 'seasoned with salt' (v. 6) suggests various ideas, including the use of salt as a preservative for food. Are the things we say worth preserving? Will they be remembered with gratitude by those we speak to? Will they make a positive difference in someone else's life?

Prayer

Lord God, may the words that I speak be a blessing to those who hear them and pleasing to you.

God's grace-giver

A friend loves at all times, and a brother is born for adversity.
PROVERBS 17:17

'If a job is worth doing, it's worth doing well' was a motto written over the blackboard at my junior school. It was wise advice that I have tried hard to follow ever since.

But how do you tackle something you don't want to do? I faced that question last week with a task I would have gladly passed on to someone else.

It was a tough job and one that needed doing, but the hardest part was knowing that it would hurt the people involved and put some close friendships at risk. I spent several uncomfortable days and nights turning over the possibilities and secretly hoping that someone else might step in and offer to take my place.

Then in the middle of a disturbing week, a parable dropped into my life. Sitting in the corner of my study was a paper mountain that had reached Mont Blanc proportions. I decided to clear the mess. Three hours later the pile had vanished and I felt the warm glow of achievement, but the best bit of all was discovering a letter I had received 18 months previously. I had put it on one side as it was one of those special, encouraging letters that we all need occasionally.

Re-reading the letter, it seemed as if it had been written a few days before. It contained some penetrating insights into the tough task I faced, even though the writer knew nothing about the circumstances. It was exactly what I needed to hear.

So what did this domestic parable teach me? First, that rotten jobs sometimes produce gems. After all, clearing up an overflowing filing tray revealed the letter that made my day. Second, that God's grace doesn't drop like a duvet from the sky. More often than not, his grace comes through human hands and feet. My letter writer took time and trouble to put thoughts into words on a page, and 18 months later those words became a bridge of grace into my life.

A famous statement in the Bible says, 'My grace is sufficient for you, for my power is made perfect in weakness' (2 Corinthians 12:9). It is a wonderful promise that has brought reassurance and strength to countless people. But the lesson I had to relearn last week is that grace is for giving as well as receiving.

It's a special calling to be a grace-giver on behalf of God.

For further reading

Acts 4:32–37; 9:26–28; 15:36–40

Joseph from Cyprus must have been a much-loved figure in the early Church, because the apostles nicknamed him Barnabas or 'Son of Encouragement'. Although he wasn't the only one to sell property and put the proceeds at the church's disposal, he is singled out here, in contrast to Ananias and Sapphira who lied about their gift. Later on, it was Barnabas who eased Saul's way into the fellowship of believers at Jerusalem, vouching for him personally while others were still distrustful and afraid. When Paul was unwilling to have Mark go with him to revisit the churches he had planted, it was Barnabas who wanted to give Mark a second chance. He was the kind of man we would all like to have as a friend—a true grace-giver.

Prayer

Thank you, Lord Jesus, for your example as the greatest grace-giver of all. As I try to follow you day by day, make me more like you.

Doorways to Praying the Lord's Prayer

Our Father in heaven,
hallowed be your name,
your kingdom come,
your will be done
on earth as it is in heaven.
Give us today our daily bread.
Forgive us our debts,
as we also have forgiven our debtors.
And lead us not into temptation,
but deliver us from the evil one.
For yours is the kingdom
and the power and the glory for ever.
Amen

Try kneeling

In the morning, O Lord, you hear my voice; in the morning I lay my requests before you and wait in expectation.
PSALM 5:3

Stuck in a ten-mile tailback on the M5 on a hot afternoon last week, I felt a twinge of sympathy for the carloads of people patiently queuing.

Inching along, we spotted a family for whom the tension looked as though it had reached crisis level. All the windows of their car were wound down to bring cooling air to some very overheated occupants. Mum and Dad gazed ahead in stony silence. In the back seat sat four small children wedged tight against each other—looking as though a death sentence hung over them. This, quite obviously, was not a precious family moment.

Then I spotted a notice in the back window, hastily scribbled in a childish hand. It simply read, 'Lord, help us and get us out of this mess!'

That is one of the best examples of a heartfelt prayer I have seen in a long time. It drew a sincere 'Amen' from the occupants of my car and brightened up a long and gloomy wait.

I have been doing some reading and thinking about the subject of prayer in recent weeks, looking particularly at what Jesus had to say about it. Prayer played an important part in his life. He often withdrew from the crowds in order to find space and time to be alone and pray. His closest followers spotted the significance of this and asked him to teach them how to pray. In response he gave them the words of what we now call The Lord's Prayer, which has become a pattern used by generations of people. Over the next few readings I want to look at this famous prayer and consider what we can learn from it.

A good starting point with prayer is to see it as a gift that all of us have been given. Like any gift, we can choose either to use it or to neglect it.

Those who choose to use it have many stories to tell, not only of remarkable answers to their prayers but also of discovering peace and an inner strength beyond themselves.

A scribbled note in the window of a car last week preached a sermon that I needed to hear. Prayer may not shift a traffic jam but it can move mountains of the heart. As one anonymous writer expressed it, 'If your problems are deep-seated or long-standing, try kneeling.'

For further reading

MARK 1:21–39

The pressures of life may drive us to prayer. On the other hand, they may get in the way of it. When we read this passage, we see that Jesus faced pressures too. Having spent the previous day preaching and healing until well into the evening, it wouldn't have been surprising if he had treated himself to a lie-in the next day! Instead he got up 'very early in the morning' (v. 35) and sought out somewhere he could be alone to pray. It wasn't long before his disciples came to look for him and the day's work began, travelling on to nearby villages for more preaching. If we have difficulty finding time to pray or are subject to interruption from others or the pressing demands of busy lives, let us try to follow Jesus' example and not be discouraged from trying again if we fail at first.

Prayer

Thank you, Lord Jesus, that you understand how hard it is at times to give prayer its rightful place in my life. Thank you for the privilege of being able to come to you just as I am, knowing that you accept me and hear me.

Almighty Father

Our Father in heaven, hallowed be your name.

MATTHEW 6:9

A teacher was taking her class through some of the names used in the Bible to describe God. One boy made an enthusiastic contribution. 'I know God's real name, Miss! It's Harold—like in the prayer, "Harold be thy name".'

I am sure the teacher was able to correct the misunderstanding—but even the right version needs some explanation.

'Our Father in heaven, hallowed be your name' is how Jesus begins what we call the Lord's Prayer. 'Hallowed' is not a word that we're used to using, but understanding it sheds a whole new light on prayer. The word means to reverence or respect someone much greater. In the case of God, it's a reminder of his majesty and purity, his total 'otherness' to ourselves.

There is a story of a young musician visiting the famous Beethoven Museum in Bonn and finding the piano on which some of the composer's greatest works had been originally played. She asked if she could play the piano—the curator agreed and the student played the opening bars of the *Moonlight Sonata*.

As she left, the student asked if any famous musicians had played this same piano that had once belonged to the great Beethoven. The curator shook his head. 'Some do, but the great Paderewiski was here a few years back and he said he was not worthy to even touch it.'

That is reverence—a recognition and respect that makes your soul walk on tiptoe. But in case we feel we are so unworthy before his greatness, Jesus puts the picture in perfect balance. 'Call him Father', he urges us, 'but never forget that he is the Holy One.'

Relationship and reverence are the twin foundations on which meaningful prayer is built. The Bible tells of God's transcendence. He is the most high God. But equally it speaks of his immanence—in Jesus he is seen as the 'most nigh' God.

All of this may sound a complicated way of approaching prayer. But in fact it is the most ground-clearing approach we can take. Instead of beginning with ourselves and what is at the top of our wish list, we are forced to stop and think. We recall who it is we come to with our needs and concerns—a heavenly Father whose nearness does not eclipse his greatness, but rather magnifies it through his embrace of grace.

For further reading

John 14:1–14

If we read through the Old Testament, we do not find any place in which God is addressed as 'Father' by his people. When Jesus taught his disciples to pray to God as their Father, it would have been a revolutionary concept because the Old Testament followers of God shrank even from naming him. Jesus consistently referred to God as his Father. God's mighty works in the Old Testament show him as an all-powerful God. Jesus shows him as our intimate, caring Father. Just as a small child's limited knowledge of her father as 'Daddy' does not deny the role he plays at work or outside the family, our knowledge of God as our Father does not make any less true the fact that he is at the same time Almighty God.

Prayer

I thank you, Almighty God, that you are my Father and that you, who hold the whole world in your hands, are interested in my small concerns.

Right on target

Your kingdom come, your will be done on earth as it is in heaven.
MATTHEW 6:10

A man had a friend who was a farmer. Walking up to his friend's house, he noticed a wooden barn, the side of which was covered in hand-painted targets. On closer inspection he noticed that each target was marked in the centre of the bullseye.

He mentioned this to the farmer, who told him that he used the wall for target practice with his crossbow. His friend congratulated him on being an excellent marksman—there was not one shot off the bullseye. 'That's on account of my special tactic,' the farmer modestly replied. 'What's that?' enquired the friend. 'Well, I find a bit of blank wall, then shoot the arrow, and wherever it lands I paint the target round it!'

I've met plenty of people who live like that. They aim at nothing and manage to hit it every time. When we look at the second phrase of the prayer Jesus taught his followers, we find the bullseye already painted in for us. 'Your kingdom come, your will be done on earth as it is in heaven.'

The target of effective prayer is that God's kingdom may come and God's will may be done. I find that a stark contrast to my breathless shopping-list of prayers, when I rush to God rather like a dash around the supermarket ten minutes before closing.

By focusing my prayers the way Jesus taught, I discover three important things.

First, when I don't know what to pray for a certain person or situation, this phrase gives me clarity. I may not know all the details, but by a simple prayer of faith I can ask for the will of God to be worked out according to his plan.

Second, I discover a great sense of security. Rather like checking your watch when hearing the familiar chimes of Big Ben, we align ourselves, our needs and our desires to the Timekeeper of the universe.

Third, I am reminded of my responsibility. To pray, 'Your kingdom come, your will be done' is not an easy option. God chooses to grow his kingdom and fulfil his will through fallible people. Often we are called to put legs on our prayers. Why pray for the hungry to be fed unless we are willing to share our own bread?

In short, if prayer is an arrow, then this powerful little phrase is the bullseye.

For further reading

ACTS 1:15–26

Finding God's will for our lives seems daunting at times. We want to do God's will but what that is doesn't seem clear. In this passage the disciples did several things which culminated in discovering who it was that God wanted to replace Judas as an apostle. First Peter interpreted and applied scripture (v. 20). Then the company of believers proposed two men and prayed that God would show them which was the man of his choosing, acknowledging that only God can 'know everyone's heart' (vv. 23–25). Then they cast lots, trusting God to influence the way they fell (v. 26). This is not a set pattern for the way in which to discern God's will in any given situation but an indication that God unfolds his will to us through many different means, and we need not fear being misled if we can sincerely pray, 'Your will be done.'

Prayer

Lord, I trust you to show me your will in my life, because I want to please you. Thank you for your word, the Bible, for godly people whose advice I can ask and for your gentle leading each step of the way, even when I do not know what the eventual outcome will be.

God's provision

Written 7 October 2000

Give us today our daily bread.

MATTHEW 6:11

As the political conference season closed this week, I was reminded that politicians are not the only ones who trade in clichés. Fine-sounding phrases are simply ladders by which we try to climb to the ideals we claim. It's whether we mean what we say that counts.

Christians are not immune to clichés. This is often seen in the prayers we pray—like the man at the weekly church prayer meeting who prayed fervently, 'Lord, blow away the cobwebs from our hearts.' One fellow worshipper became so impatient at having heard the same mindless phrase for years that he stood and prayed, 'Lord, please just kill the spider!'

Looking at the prayer Jesus taught his followers, we reach the memorable phrase, 'Give us today our daily bread'.

The whole prayer breaks down into seven specific requests, or petitions, for God to act. The first three are all to do with God—his glory and will. The last four are to do with us.

It's remarkable that Jesus taught us to pray in one breath for the great purposes of God to be achieved and in the next to ask for our daily needs to be met—from the mega to the micro in one step. But that's in tune with all he taught about a heavenly Father who is concerned about the details of our lives. According to Jesus, even the hairs of our head are numbered. This figure of speech is another way of saying that the things about ourselves that we don't know (or can't understand) are not hidden to God.

There's nothing as basic as our 'daily bread', and those things that we need to get by are not beyond the care and concern of a Father who controls the universe.

The struggle, I find, is making sure I know the difference between a need and a want. Centuries ago, a Christian leader called Gregory of Nyssa wrote:

So we say to God: Give us bread… We do not say, give us a prominent position in assemblies or monuments and statues raised to us, nor silken robes and musicians at meals, nor any other things by which the soul is estranged from the thought of God and higher things; no—but only bread!

Bread for the coming day. Not so much a cliché—more a statement of faith.

For further reading

Exodus 16:11–30; Mark 4:19

Instead of bringing their worries to God about having enough food to eat, the Israelites grumbled to Moses. God miraculously and graciously provided what they needed, even making provision for them to refrain from collecting food on the Sabbath by providing enough for two days on the sixth day. Each day there was neither too little nor too much for their needs (v. 18). Nevertheless, some of the people tried to store the manna, with disgusting results. It is always tempting to make provision for an uncertain future, but God knows our future. We can trust him each day to provide us with all that we need. It is not wrong to use wisely what he gives us today to plan and provide for tomorrow, but we are foolish if we make future security our main goal and neglect God's priorities for us.

Prayer

The King of love my Shepherd is,
Whose goodness faileth never;
I nothing lack if I am his
And he is mine for ever.

HENRY WILLIAMS BAKER (1821–77)

Empty your rucksack

Forgive us our debts, as we also have forgiven our debtors.
MATTHEW 6:12

Imagine climbing a mountain carrying a rucksack. Imagine that every few hundred yards a small stone is added to the bag. Imagine how far you would get. Better still, imagine how far you *wouldn't* get.

When Jesus taught his disciples a pattern for prayer, he included a sentence about carrying heavy loads: 'Forgive us our debts, as we also have forgiven our debtors'.

Most of us accept that we get things wrong, sometimes badly wrong. In this double-handed phrase we see the importance of seeking God's forgiveness while, at the same time, being willing to offer the hand of forgiveness to others. In my own experience, I don't find it hard to pray the first part; it's the second that's so hard. In the words of C.S. Lewis, 'Everyone says forgiveness is a lovely idea until he has something to forgive.'

But Jesus made it clear—don't bother looking for the forgiveness of God unless you are prepared to do the same for those who have wronged you.

Frederick William I was King of Prussia. He disliked his brother-in-law, the English King George II. As Frederick lay dying in 1740, his chaplain urged him to forgive all his enemies in order to pass from this life with a clear conscience. Frederick instructed his wife, 'Write to your brother and tell him that I forgive him. But be sure not to do it until after my death!'

There is something less than generous about that. Forgiveness that is genuine comes from the heart, with a willingness to bury the hatchet. And, as someone once put it, don't leave the handle sticking out for future use.

That brings us back to the heavy rucksack. Every time we miss the opportunity to put things right with God, or to release others into the gift of our forgiveness, we add another stone to the load. One of the secrets of the power of prayer is that we can find both the gift of forgiveness for our own failures and the gift of being able to forgive others for theirs. Learning how to 'empty the bag' makes our load lighter and the journey easier.

As one anonymous writer expressed it, 'We are most like beasts when we kill. We are most like men when we judge. We are most like God when we forgive.'

For further reading

PHILEMON 8–21

Forgiveness is sometimes more than ceasing to hold someone's wrong against them. Just as receiving God's forgiveness for our sins opens the way for a relationship with him as our Father, when we forgive others it may open the way for even better relationships than before, as this passage in Philemon suggests. Onesimus doesn't seem to have been a particularly 'valuable' slave: Paul says, 'Formerly he was useless to you.' Now, though, 'he has become useful', so much so that Paul would have liked to keep him around to help him (v. 13). Paul is sending him back, not as a chastened slave but 'as a dear brother' (v. 16). If Philemon will welcome Onesimus back with forgiveness, their relationship will be on a totally different basis than before. How Philemon responded to Paul's letter is left to our imagination, but Paul was 'confident' that he would 'do even more than I ask' (v. 21). Forgiveness is not always just a case of putting down a heavy load of hurt and resentment; sometimes it opens a way for God to heap even more blessing upon us.

Prayer

Ask God to show you if there is anyone in your life whom you need to forgive or any resentments or bad feelings that you need to leave behind. Ask him to help you move on in faith and, where possible, to make even better relationships than you had before.

Trials and temptations

And lead us not into temptation, but deliver us from the evil one.
MATTHEW 6:13

I have just spent a wet and soggy lunch hour on a Plymouth quayside. I was there to wish *bon voyage* to about a dozen brave people setting out on a sponsored sail across the Bay of Biscay to the Canaries.

The magnificent 67-foot *Global Challenge* yacht that will be their home for the next ten days or so is an impressive vessel with an expert skipper, but all the team know that they face some big tests through the crossing. Each crew member has paid for the privilege of joining the team and, in addition, each will raise much-needed funds for a variety of organizations dedicated to alleviating suffering.

I've found it hard to concentrate on much else this afternoon as I've thought of the challenges faced by this amateur crew.

It so happens that we reach the phrase in the Lord's Prayer that says, 'And lead us not into temptation, but deliver us from the evil one.' What was in Jesus' mind when he taught his followers this model for prayer?

It comes immediately after the phrase that speaks of our need of forgiveness and our willingness to forgive others. But is Jesus suggesting that God puts temptations in our way? In fact, the word can mean either 'testing' or 'temptation' and, as experience shows, the two are often not that far apart.

The Bible is clear about the fact that God is not the author of temptation (see James 1:13–15). Rather, it is the magnetic pull of human nature that drags us down to the lowest point.

This is a simple, heartfelt request that God would deliver us from falling to temptation or allowing any part of our lives to come under the influence of evil.

As I watched the *Global Challenge* yacht making its way into the

Plymouth Sound this afternoon, I realized that the crew face a few tests in the coming days. I trust they will come through them all safe and sound, but they will be better human beings for the experience. Teamwork, resilience, courage, endurance, patience, a sense of humour—the list of 'positives' is a long one.

It's the same principle on the voyage of life. Testings and temptations rise up like a force nine gale, but in God's hands they can deepen our faith and enrich our character.

Purity may not be popular but it is immensely powerful.

For further reading

JAMES 1:12–21

When Jesus taught his disciples to pray, 'Lead us not into temptation, but deliver us from the evil one', he wasn't telling us to pray these words 'just in case'. He knew that trials and temptations are part of being human. In verses 14 and 15, James describes sin and its consequences as following on from being 'dragged away and enticed' by our own 'evil desire'. Certain circumstances make us more likely to sin. What causes a problem for one person may not cause a problem for someone else. We need to recognize for ourselves what kind of temptations are most likely to entice us, and avoid them. It's no good praying this part of the Lord's Prayer if we're going to get up from our prayer and go straight into situations, which we could avoid, where we are going to be tempted. We can't blame God for our temptation or sin. In Ephesians 4:27 Paul tells us, 'Do not give the devil a foothold.' When we are tempted we need to deal with it there and then, because God will deliver us if we want him to.

Prayer

Help me, Lord God, to recognize those things that would make me more likely to sin, so that I can avoid them. And in those trials that I am unable to avoid, help me to persevere so that I will receive 'the crown of life' that you have promised (James 1:12).

Great is the Lord

Written in October 2000.

For yours is the kingdom and the power and the glory for ever.
Amen.

MATTHEW 6:13 (FOOTNOTE)

People make mistakes. That message has come through loud and clear
this week. Lord Phillips' report into the BSE crisis has exposed a catalogue of failures by a long list of people who should have done better.

The Russian naval bosses were further exposed as less than com-
petent in a letter revealing that at least 23 men survived the initial
explosion on board the doomed *Kursk* submarine. This has further
challenged the Russian navy's slowness to act when the disaster first
occurred.

Then we are told that the airline policy of stacking seats close together
on long-haul flights may cause deep vein thrombosis, which is thought
to have led to the tragic death of one young woman recently landed after
a 20-hour flight from Australia.

Today we reach the final part of the prayer that Jesus taught his
followers. In the Lord's Prayer we discover a pattern for all prayer, so it
is important to notice how it concludes: 'For yours is the kingdom and
the power and the glory for ever. Amen.'

The prayer finishes on a note of praise and adoration to the God who
made us. Reading through the whole of the Lord's Prayer, we notice that
it starts and ends with God—his purpose, his glory and the progress of
his kingdom. That does not mean that our daily needs are unimportant.
It simply sets them in the right balance. Start and end with God and
everything falls into place.

But what is the point of praise? If God is so great and powerful, why does he need to be told? Does this betray some dark insecurity in the divine personality? Good point —and one that deserves more than a few column inches to answer it. But if it is true that people were made by God in order to enjoy him, then worship can be seen as the fulfilment of that goal. Instead of drifting through life as stateless refugees, we can live as people with a home and a hope.

In a wonderful put-down, Churchill once commented on a rival's speech as possessing 'great humility', then mischievously added, 'and the Honourable Gentleman has much to be humble about'.

This week's headlines carry the same stark message. We have much to be humble about. But as this final phrase of the Lord's Prayer reminds us, there is nothing little about God.

For further reading

1 CHRONICLES 16:8–36

This psalm was written by David to mark a time of great rejoicing as the ark of God had been brought back to Jerusalem. It details God's faithfulness to his chosen nation, Israel. The ark of the covenant had great significance for the Israelites because it contained the tablets of the Ten Commandments and symbolized God's presence with them. It had accompanied them in their wanderings before entering the Promised Land and played a part in the crossing of the Jordan river and the fall of the walls of Jericho (Joshua 3 and 6). It had been a focus and a reminder that they were a special people for whom God had a plan and a purpose; although at that time they were not citizens of any country, they were God's citizens. Although God blessed them by giving them the Promised Land for themselves, he did not want them to be primarily concerned with an earthly kingdom, but a heavenly one. They were called to worship God and demonstrate his power in their lives, and that is what we are called to do too because, as Philippians 3:20 says, 'our citizenship is in heaven.'

Prayer

Sing to the Lord, all the earth;
proclaim his salvation day after day.
Declare his glory among the nations,
his marvellous deeds among all peoples.
For great is the Lord and most worthy of praise.
(1 Chronicles 16:23–25)

Doorways to Prayer

God speaking

Today, if you hear his voice, do not harden your hearts.
PSALM 95:7–8

Hello! You are through to the courts of heaven. To enable us to deal with your prayer effectively, please select one of the following options and register your choice by pressing the keypad on your touch-tone telephone.

- *If your prayer concerns a personal request, please press 1.*
- *If you are praying on behalf of someone else, please press 2.*
- *If you are a fully paid-up member of a recognized mainstream church, please press 3.*
- *If you are an occasional attender, please press 4.*
- *If you are a non-religious pagan, please press 5.*
- *If you are a committed atheist or agnostic taking a long shot, please press 6.*
- *If none of these options apply, please hold.*

You are in a queuing system and one of our prayer operatives will be with you shortly. Thank you for your prayer request. All of us here at the gates of heaven are working hard to deal with it as soon as we can. In the meantime, please relax and enjoy a selection of sounds from our Religious Classics Collection. Bless you for calling.

Having spent twenty minutes on the phone this week playing lottery numbers with talking machines, I would simply like to register that I'm glad prayer is not that complicated. Try this for size from the lips of the greatest expert on prayer, Jesus.

Find a quiet, secluded place so you won't be tempted to role-play before God. Just be there as simply and honestly as you can manage. The focus will shift from you to God, and you will begin to sense his grace. The world is full of so-called prayer warriors who are prayer-ignorant. They're full of formulas and programs and advice, peddling techniques for getting what you want from God. Don't fall for that nonsense. This is your Father you are dealing with, and he knows better than you what you need. With a God like this loving you, you can pray very simply.

MATTHEW 6:6–8 (*THE MESSAGE*)

Thankfully, the courts of heaven are not hard to contact, and you don't need a touch-tone phone, just a hungry heart.

For further reading

PSALM 66:17–20; MATTHEW 6:5–8

Prayer is, quite simply, about communicating with God, and communication is two-way. Just as much as we want God to hear us when we pray, we need to be able to hear him. When we are living with a clear conscience, prayer is straightforward with nothing to hinder it, but when we allow sin to creep into our lives, God's voice becomes fainter. This is why, when we are tempted and open the door to giving in, even just a crack, the temptation calls ever more strongly and we no longer hear God plainly. It is not that he is no longer there but that we have hardened our heart and turned our back on him. But God is our loving, merciful Father and if we repent of our hardness of heart and turn back to him we will be able to say with the writer of Psalm 66, 'Praise be to God, who has not rejected my prayer or withheld his love from me' (v. 20).

Prayer

Father, I want to feel at home in your presence, hearing your voice and knowing that you hear me.

Power to plod

Then Jesus told his disciples a parable to show them that they should always pray and not give up.
LUKE 18:1

If you had to guess which was faster, would it be a greyhound or a racing pigeon?

The matter was decided recently in an unusual contest held at a Wimbledon stadium. Althea Storm, a four-year-old greyhound, emerged the winner over Speckled Jim, a five-year-old racing pigeon. By all accounts it was a close thing, with the dog leading by just one second as it crossed the line at the end of the 80-metre course.

'What's the point?' you may well ask. Apart from generating a fair bit of income for the bookmakers and winning punters, an important scientific argument was (apparently) settled.

But that all presupposes that faster equals better, which seems a cardinal rule in our high-speed society—and I am not so sure that it is true.

As the Bible expresses it, 'The race is not to the swift or the battle to the strong, nor does food come to the wise or wealth to the brilliant or favour to the learned; but time and chance happen to them all' (Ecclesiastes 9:11).

One of the predictable things about life is its unpredictability, which means that the fastest may not always turn out to be the winner of the race.

The old fable of the tortoise and the hare reminds us that plodders often cross the finish-line first. Patience, determination and 'stickability' may be forgotten virtues but they are stock-in-trade for those who may not be quick but who never quit.

It was brought home to me today as I read of the famous meeting between Stanley and Livingstone back in 1871. The explorer had been sent to find the missionary and, having achieved his objective, spent several months with David Livingstone, observing his work.

Stanley was deeply impressed by the old man's quiet patience and dedication to his calling. He noticed his deep love for the Africans with whom he worked and the single-mindedness of his vision. Livingstone never once discussed his faith, but Stanley later wrote, 'When I saw that unwearied patience, that unflagging zeal, those enlightened sons of Africa, I became a Christian at his side, though he never spoke to me about it.' The power of a patient and committed life went further than any sermon.

So when you pray, don't ask to be faster than anyone else. Simply ask for the power to plod.

For further reading

LUKE 18:1–8; 1 CORINTHIANS 3:6–9

It's not necessarily correct to conclude that when God does not answer a prayer quickly he is never going to do it, so we should give up praying. Jesus told this memorable parable in Luke 18 to teach the disciples and us not to be discouraged but to be persistent in prayer. Like the widow in the parable, we come to God with no bargaining power but, *unlike* the judge, God does care about us and about what concerns us. Have you been praying for a long time, perhaps for many years, for someone you love to come to know the truth of the gospel in their own life? Have there been times when your hopes have been raised but time has passed and there has been no apparent change after all? Don't be discouraged. Don't stop praying and hoping. Don't give up. We may be mistaken in thinking that God is not acting because we cannot see the work he is doing in a person's heart. This is all the more reason to keep on praying and being faithful and consistent in the way we ourselves live.

Prayer

Bring before God again those you regularly pray for who do not know him. Thank him for those you have prayed for in the past who have responded to his love.

Are you listening?

God is in heaven and you are on earth so let your words be few.
ECCLESIASTES 5:2

Can silence be heard? This question ran through my mind a few nights ago. Unable to sleep in the sticky heat, I opened the windows wide for some cool air. Being in the depths of the French countryside miles from the nearest town, there was nothing to disturb the sound of silence.

Lying there gazing into a perfectly still night sky, my ears pricked up at unfamiliar sounds grumbling at the edges of the quietness. I struggled to identify what they were. Was that a cricket, or someone moving about the house? Was a tap dripping somewhere? I began to realize how noisy silence can be.

Thinking later about my sleepless night, I wondered how I could find that magical silence again—not just to find it, but somehow to hold on to it and keep it safe as a private treasure.

One of the heroes of the Bible is a man called Elijah. He was called to be God's spokesman at a dark time in Israel's history. His role caused him to stand against a corrupt royal family, and an avalanche of hostile popular opinion and religious beliefs. He was a strong man who did a good job.

But even the strongest falter. One day, in bleak despair, Elijah turned his back on his calling and ran away. He wanted to die and bluntly told God that he had nothing left to give.

What happened next offers an insight into God's ways of doing business with people. There was no sermon, damning rebuke or encouraging pep talk—just silence, some good food, rest and a six-week break, after which Elijah found himself at a mountain called Sinai. And at that significant place God drew close to reveal something new to someone who thought he knew it all.

We are told of an earthquake, a strong wind and fire, but God didn't reveal himself in any of these powerful forces. After all three had passed, there came what is described as a 'gentle whisper' (1 Kings 19:12). In the stillness God spoke and Elijah listened and grew.

Silence does have a sound and a language all its own, and, as Elijah discovered, it is a language that God appears to favour.

Thomas Carlyle was not far off the bullseye when he wrote, 'Silence is deep as eternity, speech as shallow as time.'

Find the silence, and prize it greatly.

For further reading

ECCLESIASTES 5:1–7

We are not always ready to listen to God. Part of the problem is our preoccupation with our own needs and concerns. When we come to pray to God, our minds are busy with so many things, and it is hard to put them aside and be open to what God wants to say to us. Perhaps we haven't experienced anything like the wind, earthquake and fire, but sometimes it takes something fairly drastic for God to get our full attention. Ecclesiastes offers some wise instruction on how to approach God: 'Do not be quick with your mouth, do not be hasty in your heart to utter anything before God' (v. 2). We are specifically warned against making promises to God that we will be unable to keep, because this will displease him. Jesus talked about the foolishness of thinking that the more we say, the better our prayers will be heard (Matthew 6:7). The truth is that the better we listen, the more we will know how we should pray.

Prayer

Has God been trying to get your attention? Ask him if there is anything he wants to say to you and then spend a few minutes being quiet and listening for his 'gentle whisper'.

If you haven't prayed, don't criticize!

Written in 1997 after Labour's election victory.

I urge, then, first of all, that requests, prayers, intercession and thanksgiving be made for everyone—for kings and all those in authority.

1 TIMOTHY 2:1–2

Whichever way you voted in the General Election, it's hard to deny that the final outcome looks like change with a capital 'C'.

This week the Queen's Speech set out a radical agenda for the coming years. Promises are what elections are made of; government requires steadier nerves. Bismarck said, 'Politics is the art of the possible.' As Tony Blair acknowledged on entering Downing Street, now comes the hard part.

Christians are encouraged to pray for those who lead in national affairs and, every Sunday, from church to chapel, prayers are offered in obedience to God's direction. I still struggle with the stark command: 'Submit yourselves for the Lord's sake to every authority instituted among men: whether to the king, as the supreme authority, or to governors, who are sent by him to punish those who do wrong and to commend those who do right' (1 Peter 2:13–14). My struggle is that the words were written when the 'king' was the evil Emperor Nero, and the person who wrote them was martyred for his faith not long afterwards.

The challenge is to pray for those who lead, whether or not you agree with their policies, and to do everything possible to uphold good order in society. But how should we pray for those who govern?

Harry Truman was serving as Vice-President of the USA when Franklin D. Roosevelt died a few months after winning his fourth term as President. Truman found himself thrust into the office of the Presidency with mixed emotions.

A close friend took Truman aside and gave him a piece of valuable advice. 'From here on out, you're going to have lots of people around you. They'll try to put up a wall around you and cut you off from any ideas but theirs. They'll tell you what a great man you are, Harry. But you and I both know you ain't.'

Prime Minister Blair and his ministers need our prayers not because of the colour of their party but because of the weight of responsibility they carry. And if you are stuck for what to pray on their behalf, here are two suggestions for starters—humility as they carry out their tasks, and honest friends like the one who promised Harry Truman that he would never let him forget the real man behind the public image.

For further reading

PSALM 101:1–8

When we read the psalms of David, we may forget that he was a king, but in this psalm we can see what made him a good ruler—his seeking after God (v. 2) and his desire to lead a blameless life and to surround himself with people of similar integrity (vv. 6–7). We know that David didn't always get it right and sometimes sinned disastrously. When we hear today of politicians doing wrong, it is very easy to criticize and condemn, but perhaps we should examine ourselves. Have we prayed for them that they will be able to resist when temptation comes their way, as it probably will? As they try to keep their election promises and as they respond to events that are outside their control, are our prayers upholding them? It is sometimes said that those who neglect to vote forfeit the right to criticize the government of the day. The same could be said of those of us who neglect to pray.

Prayer

Lord, we bring before you those who govern us, asking that you will encourage and strengthen them as they seek to do what is right, and that you would restrain them when they act unwisely or wrongly. Protect them from harm in our violent world and lift them up when they feel discouraged or unappreciated despite their hard work.

Any questions?

Ask and it will be given to you; seek and you will find; knock and the door will be opened to you.

MATTHEW 7:7

A man telephoned a friend and a small child answered the phone.

'Can I speak to Mummy or Daddy, please?' the man asked. 'No,' came the whispered reply, 'they're busy.'

'Well, is your brother or sister there?' the man persisted. 'No,' said the child, 'they're busy too.'

The caller tried again: 'Is there anyone else I can speak to?' The line was silent for a moment, then the child whispered, 'There are two policemen downstairs.' By now the man was worried. 'Let me speak to one of them,' he said. 'I can't,' the child replied. 'They're busy as well.'

Imagining some dire emergency, the caller tried to humour the youngster. 'Sounds like an interesting time in your house if everyone is so busy. What are they all doing?' Another pause. 'They're looking for me,' was the quiet response.

I have been doing a fair amount of searching over the past few weeks. Whoever said that problems are like buses—none for ages, then several come along at once—knew what they were talking about. I have been struggling to find answers to several large, unconnected problems.

I occasionally meet people who believe they have a hotline to heaven. Every problem has an answer: all you need to do is pray and watch the result come tumbling into your lap. I have no doubt about the power of prayer but, somehow, I am not sure the automatic slot machine approach is always right. Often answers don't come easily but are forged through the furnace of affliction. As the old Jewish proverb puts it, 'Tears are to the soul what soap is to the body.'

In times of searching, it is good to be reminded of the many promises in the Bible that speak of God's desire to give wisdom and insight to those prepared to look hard. Some words that have brought peace and encouragement to many come from the book of Proverbs:

If you accept my words and store up my commands within you, turning your ear to wisdom and applying your heart to understanding, and if you call aloud for insight and cry aloud for understanding, and if you look for it as silver and search for it as for hidden treasure, then you will understand the fear of the Lord and find the knowledge of God.

PROVERBS 2:1–5

Searching for answers stretches the mind and strengthens the soul.

For further reading

JOHN 3:1–10; LUKE 7:18–23; MARK 11:27–33

Jesus was asked many questions during his life on earth, and his response each time was tailored to the needs and motives of the questioner. Nicodemus probably went away feeling even more confused than when he had first come to Jesus. It would take time, and the death and resurrection of Jesus, before he could fully understand what he had been told.

When John the Baptist, discouraged and in prison, sent his disciples to find out if Jesus was really the one for whom he had been preparing the way, Jesus sent them back to cite the evidence of all that was happening in fulfilment of prophecy, and with a personal message of encouragement to John: 'Blessed is the man who does not fall away on account of me' (Luke 7:23).

The Pharisees were looking for an excuse to condemn Jesus and their question was the means to that end (Mark 11:28). If they had been willing to commit themselves and answer Jesus' question, would he have answered them? As it was, he refused.

When we go to God with our problems and questions, we can be sure that if we sincerely want an answer he will not be deaf to our prayers. Even if he doesn't answer immediately or in the way we expect, he does not want us to be discouraged. We may not immediately appreciate what his answer means, but if we continue to seek him he will make it plain.

Prayer

Thank you, Lord, that your 'eyes… are on the righteous and [your] ears are attentive to their prayer' (1 Peter 3:12).

Tense times

From the ends of the earth I call to you, I call as my heart grows faint;
lead me to the rock that is higher than I.

PSALM 61:2

An interviewer conducted a travel survey on a cross-Channel ferry. Her speech was slurred because she'd visited the dentist that morning and the effects of an injection were still wearing off. She interviewed a passenger who told her, rather coyly, that she was on her honeymoon. As the interview concluded, the passenger asked why she had been chosen out of a boat full of travellers. 'We speak to every tenth person coming up the stairs,' she was told. Her face dropped. 'Did I look that tense?' she asked.

Whether or not we show it, stress plays a part in all our lives in one way or another. According to an American survey, as many as 90 per cent of visits to doctors in the USA are stress-related.

As a doctor once explained to me, though, stress is the body's natural reaction to a challenge, and should not always be seen as a bad thing in itself. If managed properly, it can help us tackle things we might not otherwise be able to face.

I often meet people whose lives are dominated by stress and who live with the costly consequences—and they are not the only ones who pick up the bill, as those who live with them will freely admit.

I have recently read a book entitled *Too Busy Not To Pray* (IVP, 1989). Its author, Bill Hybels, admits to having lived life in the fast lane for too long before discovering the deep inner peace that comes through the practice of prayer. We need to learn to slow down and walk at God's pace. He writes:

No one can become an authentic Christian on a steady diet of activity. Power comes out of stillness; strength comes out of solitude. Decisions that change the entire course of your life come out of the Holy of Holies, your times of stillness before God.

The book of Psalms is a kaleidoscope of faith. It's a prayer book made from the raw material of human experience, including times of darkness, doubt and difficulty. King David, who composed many psalms, knew times of stress. But he also knew where to go, what to do and who to call when times were tense: 'From the ends of the earth I call to you, I call as my heart grows faint; lead me to the rock that is higher than I.'

For further reading

PSALM 142:1–7

The situation was tense. David was on the run from King Saul's murderous rage. He had taken refuge in a cave where he was joined by his family and a large group of those 'who were in distress or in debt or discontented' (1 Samuel 22:1–2). He wasn't alone but he felt as though he were. He felt that no one cared about him and that he wasn't safe anywhere (Psalm 142:4), so he poured out his troubles and distress to God. In the narrative in 1 Samuel we find that God spoke to David through the prophet Gad, telling him where to go next. We may find ourselves in situations where we do not know which way to turn. We may feel that the pressures on us are hard to bear but, like David, we can find our 'refuge' in God. Spending time with him will give us the strength to carry on and remind us that we are not alone. We don't need to put on an act or pretend to him that we are coping, because he already knows what we are feeling and accepts us just as we are. Even if life is not particularly tough at the moment, taking time each day to get to know God better will prepare us for whatever that day may hold.

Prayer

Thank you that I can come to you and pour out the troubles of my heart. My soul finds rest in you and my hope comes from you (Psalm 62:5).

Doorways to Discipleship

Richer together, poorer apart

But in fact God has arranged the parts in the body, every one of them, just as he wanted them to be.

1 CORINTHIANS 12:18

My patient, hard-working secretary, Karen, has left me for pastures new. In the weeks before her departure she pinned the following piece on the office noticeboard. Personally, I put it down to demob spirit.

Ten Reasons Why God Made Eve

1. God worried that Adam would get lost in the garden because men never ask directions.
2. Adam needed someone to hand him the television remote control because men never want to see what's on the box, they want to see what else is on.
3. Adam would never get a new fig leaf when the seat wore out and would need someone to buy one.
4. God knew that Adam would never make a doctor's appointment for himself.
5. God knew that Adam would never remember which day to put the rubbish out.
6. God knew that if the world was to be populated, men would never cope with childbirth.
7. As 'keeper of the garden', Adam would never remember where he'd left his tools.
8. The scriptural account of creation suggests that Adam would always need someone else to blame.
9. The Bible says, 'It is not good for man to be alone', suggesting that men left to themselves get into trouble.

10. When God finished creating Adam, he stood back and said, 'I can do better than that!'

For all the jokes about the battle of the sexes, what a dull world it would be if we all looked and acted the same. The truth is that God made us different for a reason. Men and women bear the divine image as well as carrying the down-side of a human nature that is both fallen and marred.

Sadly, the church has not had a great track record through the centuries in recognizing the equality of the sexes. Male chauvinism is a sin that remains deeply rooted in our culture and can be as damaging as any form of sectarianism.

A verse in the New Testament says, 'Do not think of yourself more highly than you ought, but rather think of yourself with sober judgment' (Romans 12:3). It's followed by a plea for Christians to recognize that the human body is made up of different parts, so a balanced church makes room for people with different skills and gifts.

Richer together, poorer apart: that seems like a healthy starting point in understanding and enjoying the differences between the sexes.

For further reading

1 CORINTHIANS 12:12–27

We need to remember that we live in a society with warped values. In God's sight, earthly distinctions do not apply; each member of his Church has a crucial role to play if the body is to function to his glory. But we may still be tempted to apply the world's standards to the Church and to ourselves. Verses 15 and 16 of this passage describe the kind of things we say to ourselves when we feel that the part we have to play is inferior to other people's. If we complain in this way we are really complaining against God, because he has equipped us and placed us where he wants us (v. 18). Verse 21 describes what we sometimes say to each other. How wrong we are! We are all 'indispensable'. Verses 25 and 26 tell us that we are to treat each other with equal concern, entering into each other's joys and sorrows, remembering that God made each one of us unique for a reason.

Prayer

Pray whichever prayer applies to you:

Lord, there are times when I feel inferior to other people in my church. Whatever they do is successful and they seem to have the Christian life all worked out. Help me to find the part you want me to play in the church and to do it for you and not for the praise of other people.

Lord, I often look around and want to tell other people what they ought to be doing in the church. Help me to remember that you have 'arranged the parts in the body, every one of them, just as [you] wanted them to be'. Keep me from feeling superior to people whose gifts, humanly speaking, don't seem as important or as effective as mine.

Lookalikes and stereotypes

Then [Jesus] said to [Peter], 'Follow me.'
JOHN 21:19

Like them or loathe them, or do all that you can to avoid them, computers are here to stay. Our lives are bound up with those demanding little machines, even if we don't own one and have vowed never to learn how they work.

A computer expert from a naval background had learned that the correct way to refer to a ship was as 'she'. But what puzzled him was that computers seemed to possess no gender. So he set a group of colleagues a test: is a computer male or female?

He split them into two groups, one male and the other female. This is what they concluded. The women's group believed that computers were definitely masculine and should be referred to as 'he/him'. In support of their case they cited:

- In order to get their attention you have to turn them on.
- They have a lot of data but remain clueless.
- They try to solve your problems but half the time they *are* the problem.
- As soon as you commit to one, you realize that if you'd waited a bit longer you could have had a better model.

The men concluded that computers were definitely female because:

- No one but the creator understands their internal logic.
- The language they use to communicate with others of their kind is incomprehensible to anyone else.

- Even your smallest mistakes are stored in the long-term memory for later retrieval.
- As soon as you make a commitment to one, you find yourself spending half your wages on accessories for it.

I was in a meeting recently when the topic of how men and women approach tasks was discussed. After a few light-hearted jibes along the lines of the computer experts' conclusions, we got down to a more serious discussion. We concluded that men and women do approach things differently, but that is something we should see as a strength, not a weakness.

In the opening chapter of the first book of the Bible we read, 'So God created man in his own image, in the image of God he created him, male and female he created them' (Genesis 1:27).

As human beings we reflect the image—and the glory—of the one who created us. And that *includes* the differences.

For further reading

John 21:15–22

When Jesus said, 'You will stretch out your hands' (v. 18), Peter would have understood that Jesus was saying that he too would undergo crucifixion. It could not have been welcome news and it must have been hard for Peter to take in. So he tried to change the subject by looking at John and asking, 'What about him?' Jesus replied that John's future was not Peter's concern: 'You must follow me' (v. 22). Each one of us is God's unique creation. We're not even limited editions, but one-offs, never to be repeated, and we are called to be Christ-like. Why, then, do we so often look around and compare ourselves to other Christians, aspiring to be like them, or criticizing them for not being like us? God has a unique plan for the life of each one of us. We should not be overly concerned with how he has called others to serve him, but should seek to find his will for our own life and obey it.

Prayer

The task your wisdom has assigned
O let me cheerfully fulfil,
In all my works your presence find,
And prove your good and perfect will.

CHARLES WESLEY (1707–88)

Cracked pots

But we have this treasure in jars of clay to show that this all-surpassing power is from God and not from us.

2 CORINTHIANS 4:7

It's official. I am a crackpot.

I recently sat a psychometric test, and yesterday a nice man talked me through the results for a couple of hours. I won't bore you with the details other than to say that the findings were uncannily accurate. My wife read the 20-page report and concluded, 'They've got you in one', then muttered furtively about how she could add a few pages of her own observations. But enough of that.

At least it solves my Christmas present problem, as I'm thinking of giving all my friends and family a copy of the report in the hope that everyone will understand me better in the coming year. Some hope!

It is unnerving to read in black and white some accurate descriptions of how I respond to different situations, but it is also very useful to know how I might do better in the future.

This week I was reminded of the story of an Indian water carrier who every morning took two large pots to the well. He carried them home, one at each end of a long pole. The problem was that one of the pots was cracked and by the time he returned from the well at least half of its contents had leaked away. According to the story, the defective pot was in deep despair one day and told the carrier that he needed to find a replacement. 'I'm useless,' it exclaimed. 'I never do my job properly. You need to find a better pot.'

The carrier spoke with reassurance. 'Have you never noticed the flowers that grow at the side of the path to the well? Because I knew about your flaw, I planted seeds there. Every day as we return I carry you on that side of the path, and as we walk, you water them. How else could I pick such beautiful flowers to adorn my master's table each day? Were you not the way you are, the master would not have had such beauty to grace his house.'

The story of the pot has a point. Flaws can have their uses. The by-products of our failures can often prove to be better than the dreams of our achievements. As Jesus expressed it, 'My power is made perfect in weakness' (2 Corinthians 12:9).

Believe me, it's true. I should know. I am a crackpot. It's official.

For further reading

2 CORINTHIANS 3:18—4:15

Christians are called to reflect Christ's glory as we become more and more like him (3:18) so that many more people will come to know him for themselves (4:15). Of what use would we be to him if we were to display our own 'glory'? It is not our persuasive arguments and attractive, successful lives that draw others to Jesus, but God shining his light in their hearts and revealing himself to them as he did to us (4:5–6). Paul says that we are very ordinary vessels (clay jars) containing priceless 'treasure', which is 'the knowledge of the glory of God in the face of Christ' (4:6). It is humbling that God should be best able to work through us when we are weak and dependent on him, but we should rejoice that he chooses to do so. We do not have to trick or deceive people into believing in God. Nor do we have to try to dress up God's word so that it will be more acceptable to people. We simply have to be ourselves, telling the truth as God has revealed it to us and trusting him to do the rest.

Prayer

I am not ashamed of your gospel, Lord, because it has the power to save everyone who believes (Romans 1:16). I am willing to be a cracked pot or a clay jar for you to use.

Prophets and mosquitoes

Written 1 December 2001

You must go to everyone I send you to and say whatever I command you.

JEREMIAH 1:7

I have never met Anita Roddick, founder of the Body Shop empire, but she strikes me as an enterprising and gifted person who would be fascinating to talk with. I read a quote from her that seemed to sum up her driving ambition: 'If you think you're too small to have an impact, try going to bed with a mosquito in the room.'

Anita makes her point well. Little things and small people can make a difference. Last week, Mary Whitehouse, the veteran campaigner, died, and tributes and commentaries about her life have been circulating. It would be fair to say that she has received mixed reviews. She was someone who never evoked a neutral response—people either liked or loathed her.

I met Mary Whitehouse back in the 1980s when I was asked to interview her at a conference. She and her husband, Ernest, had asked for transport to and from the event and so it was decided that, by doubling as chauffeur and minder, I could build a rapport with her that would make the interview glide more easily.

I was not (up until then) a great fan of hers, partly because I felt that she fought some unnecessary battles and partly due to the tone of her campaigning. But I came away from that meeting with a deep impression of someone who was willing to get involved. Even though I doubted some of her tactics, I was overawed by her courage.

The part of Mary's story that is often forgotten deals with how she first stepped into the public arena. She was a schoolteacher handling the pastoral care of teenage girls. Facing the growing impact of underage sex and pregnancy, Mary turned her attention to the influence of television on patterns of behaviour.

She was a practitioner who was fed up with calling ambulances to the bottom of the cliff and suggested that we might consider building a fence at the top. The thing that spoke to me about her life was her willingness to stand up and be counted. That isn't very fashionable. We like popular causes that gain applause and boost our street cred.

But check the history books. Pioneers and prophets are never 'majority' people. We often end up building monuments to their memory out of the stones we threw at them during their lifetime.

Their role is to challenge, question and... irritate. Just like a mosquito.

For further reading

JEREMIAH 1:4–8; 20:1–12

When God called Jeremiah to be his prophet, he promised Jeremiah that he would be with him and would rescue him (1:8), but he did not promise that his life would be easy. Jeremiah's life was going to involve rejection and physical hardship, but it would have been much harder for him if he had known in advance the persecution he was to face. God protects us from worry about the future by taking us one step at a time along the road he has prepared for us. We may look at a prominent campaigner like Mary Whitehouse and be thankful that God has not called us to stand out in such a way, but there are times when we have to make a stand for what is right, perhaps in our community, at work or at church. This may be uncomfortable and painful but we can rely on God to give us the strength we need when we need it. He never calls us to do anything that he doesn't also equip us to do.

Prayer

I praise you, Lord, because you are 'with me like a mighty warrior; so my persecutors will stumble and not prevail' (Jeremiah 20:11).

God's reward

Whatever you do, work at it with all your heart, as working for the Lord, not for men.

COLOSSIANS 3:23

Oscar Hammerstein was a talented songwriter who collaborated with Richard Rodgers to produce some of the best musicals ever written. He offers an insight into his approach to work in his book, *Lyrics* (Omnibus Press, 2002). He recalls seeing a picture of the famous Statue of Liberty taken from a helicopter. He was amazed at the intricacy of the statue's hairstyle, obviously the result of some painstaking work on the part of the sculptor, who chose to omit no detail.

Hammerstein reflected that the sculptor would never have imagined that one day people would be able to use a transportation device that would allow them to study the statue from above. Yet he had given as much care to what he may have considered to be the 'invisible' part of his work as he did to the more obvious features.

Hammerstein drew an important lesson from this discovery: 'When you are creating a work of art or any other kind of work, finish the job perfectly. You never know when a helicopter, or some other instrument not at the moment invented may come along and find you out.'

We may never create a piece of work that becomes as famous as the Statue of Liberty, but Hammerstein's observation applies equally to life's small tasks. Attention to detail and faithfulness in what is unseen remain important components in a job well done.

The French religious writer Michel Quoist sums up that response in a simple meditation entitled 'The Brick' (*Prayers of Life*, Gill & MacMillan, 1963):

The Bricklayer laid a brick on the bed of cement.
Then with a precise stroke of his trowel spread another layer
And without a by-your-leave, laid on another brick.
The foundations grew visibly,
The building rose, tall and strong, to shelter men.

I thought, Lord, of that brick buried in the darkness
at the base of the big building.
No one sees it, but it accomplishes its task, and the other bricks need it.
Lord, what difference whether I am on the rooftop or in the foundations of
your building, as long as I stand faithfully at the right place?

Doing something well may not seem glamorous but it reaps a rich reward.

For further reading

MATTHEW 6:1–4; 1 CORINTHIANS 3:10–14

Jesus warned his disciples to be careful of their motives when doing good works. If they were working to impress other people, they would receive the reward they were aiming for and there would be no reward from God. Jesus implied that only those things done out of service to God would receive a reward from him. There is going to come a time when God will weigh up all that we have done—all the bricks we have laid, as it were, on the foundation of our faith in Christ—and test their quality. Although it isn't always possible to conceal from others the good things that we do, if we are motivated by the desire to please God and don't flaunt our good works, then he will be pleased with us. It is tempting to be less scrupulous about doing the things that no one else will ever know about, but God sees it all. The true test of our faithfulness is how we do those things that only God sees.

Prayer

Father, I want to serve you and please you in everything I do. I am willing to occupy whatever place you give me.

When good ideas backfire

Trust in the Lord with all your heart and lean not on your own understanding; in all your ways acknowledge him, and he will make your paths straight.

PROVERBS 3:5

A newspaper story caught my eye a few days ago. Apparently police in Bristol had been keeping a house under observation for some time, following a tip-off that it was being used for drug dealing.

Such an operation requires sensitivity and one enterprising detective hit on what seemed, at the time, a bright idea. The police approached an elderly neighbour. Would she be prepared to take the number plates of any car that parked outside the house when the owner got out and went inside? The lady was happy to oblige and said she perfectly understood the need for caution.

The detective returned after a few days for a progress report and the helpful neighbour presented him with a pile of number plates she had dutifully unscrewed from suspected vehicles. I think that's called obeying instructions to the letter!

The image of this senior citizen crawling snake-like across the street with a screwdriver clamped between her teeth will live with me for a long time—and I hope she gets a commendation for her efforts.

'Do as you're told' is something we hear from our earliest days, and some of us respond to that advice with varying degrees of success or failure. Blind obedience is not always a good thing, and people who give orders sometimes turn out to be untrustworthy in the first place. But obedience and faith are very closely linked in the Bible and the message is simple: you can tell what someone believes by the way they behave.

Augustine was an influential Christian leader many centuries ago and was asked how someone could live a life that honoured God. His response was short and sharp: 'Love God and do as you please.' His point is clear: if love for God is top of our personal agenda, then everything else flows from that. Doing as I please is not a licence to kill or do anything else that takes my fancy, but once I am anchored to the priority of loving God, then doing what he wants comes before doing what I want.

I am grateful to the anonymous lady in Bristol for making me smile, but even more, for providing a fresh and thought-provoking insight into Jesus' words: 'If you love me you will obey what I command' (John 14:15).

For further reading

1 SAMUEL 4:1–11

Battle had raged between the Israelites and the Philistines, and the Israelites had come off worse. Back at camp the elders asked, 'Why did the Lord bring defeat upon us today before the Philistines?' (v. 3). Then, instead of waiting for God to answer, they came up with their own solution: if they were to fetch the ark (the visible sign of God's presence) from Shiloh, then God would be with them and they would defeat the Philistines. It seemed like a good idea at the time but it was fatally flawed. God's presence and favour did not depend on whether or not the ark was present but on whether the Israelites were obedient to him. They did not want to serve God, they wanted God to serve them—and their plan backfired in a big way. The Philistines, hearing that the ark had come into the Israelite camp, were spurred on to fight even more fiercely. Many Israelites were killed and the ark was captured. When we have a good idea, we need to make certain it is God's idea too.

Prayer

Lord, fill me with the knowledge of your will through all spiritual wisdom and understanding (Colossians 1:9).

Forgetful people

Remember, therefore, what you have received and heard; obey it and repent.

REVELATION 3:3

If you've stood in a supermarket with your mind as blank as a freshly rubbed blackboard, you won't want to meet Jonathan Hancock. In the time it takes for you to recall whether it was eggs or carrots you came in for, he will probably have memorized the contents of every shelf in every aisle.

Mr Hancock, you see, is the current world Memory Champion at the tender age of 22 and has already appeared twice in the *Guinness Book of Records*. Hailed as the 'Crown Prince of Memory', his current project is to cut the world record for recalling the order of the cards in a pack, to a staggering 28 seconds. His book (*Mind Power System*, Hodder and Stoughton, 1995) offers ways in which lesser mortals like you and I can learn to store and retrieve information in that oldest and most reliable of all computers, the brain.

I am not sure if I am beyond help, but memory damage for some goes far beyond the frustration of forgetting names or shopping lists. If you have ever nursed a friend or relative whose mind is damaged by disease, you will know how painful that experience can be; and for those who suffer from severe memory loss, we cannot begin to imagine the depth of their despair at times.

A few days ago I was brought up short with a reminder of the most serious of all types of memory loss. When human beings forget their creator, we exhibit selfishness of the worst kind. I came across some words of the famous US President, Abraham Lincoln. In 1863, a National Day of Prayer and Fasting was called and the President himself wrote the official proclamation announcing it. He wrote:

We have been the recipients of the choicest bounties of heaven. We have been preserved these many years in peace and prosperity. We have grown in numbers, wealth and power as no other nation has ever grown. But we have forgotten God. We have vainly imagined, in the deceitfulness of our heart, that all these blessings were produced by some superior wisdom and virtue of our own. Intoxicated with unbroken success, we have become too self-sufficient to feel the necessity of redeeming and preserving grace, too proud to pray to the God that made us.

May we never be guilty of forgetting the things that truly matter.

For further reading

Exodus 16:1–9

Moses had led the Israelites out of Egypt, carrying gold and silver given them by the Egyptians (Exodus 12:35–36); their children had been spared God's plague on the firstborn sons of the Egyptians (12:23); they had been led and protected by pillars of cloud and fire (13:21); and they had crossed the Red Sea on dry ground (14:22). We might expect that the Israelites' faith in God would have reached a high point, but they seem to have been forgetful. They started to wonder where their next meal would come from. Then they began to think that life in Egypt hadn't been so bad, after all, and they grumbled against Moses and Aaron. As Moses pointed out, they were really grumbling against God (16:7). When we face difficulties, do we complain or do we turn to God, trusting him for help? Have we seen God work in the past but doubt that he will do so right now? We can learn from the Israelites and, when faced with a problem, remember with thankfulness how God has helped us in the past and ask him to help us again.

Prayer

Lord, you were so patient with the Israelites and you are so patient with me. Help me to remember all that you have done for me so that when problems arise I will turn to you for help and not grumble.

No looking back

Written in April 2001.

As the time approached for him to be taken up to heaven, Jesus resolutely set out for Jerusalem.
LUKE 9:51

If you have struggled to find a piece of good news this week, let me pass some on.

Polio, once a feared disease, is now almost eradicated. According to a report from the World Health Organization, cases have fallen by 99 per cent since 1998, and the year 2000 saw only 3,500 reported cases worldwide. Sadly, there are still 20 countries where the disease is active, but according to Gro Harlem, Director General of the WHO, 'Victory over the polio virus is in sight.' And that was an unthinkable prospect only a few years ago.

The goal is that by 2005 polio will have been totally eradicated, and it seems a realistic target. The victory over polio has been won through a dedicated immunization campaign involving 550 million children in 82 countries. It has required close co-operation between national and international agencies and the vital fund-raising work of charities such as Rotary International.

Such a heartening story reminds me of several truths. First, we should never give up on a so-called hopeless case; second, co-operation can achieve brilliant results; and third, some battles are worth fighting all the way.

It so happens that this week I came across a quote from US President Franklin Roosevelt. He was struck down with polio as an adult and, after a long struggle and with the support of his wife, he made it back into politics. When asked about his energy and determination, he replied, 'You're looking at a man who spent two years trying to wiggle his big toe.'

Winston Churchill, who epitomized the spirit of dogged perseverance, once wrote, 'Never give in, never give in—never, never, never, never—in nothing, great or small, large or petty—never give in except to convictions of honour and good sense.'

Without doubt, many of the world's greatest accomplishments owe as much to persistence as to brilliance.

Every Easter we are reminded of the greatest example of all when it comes to single-minded determination in the fight against the world's deadliest disease: 'Let us fix our eyes on Jesus, the author and perfecter of our faith, who for the joy set before him endured the cross, scorning its shame, and sat down at the right hand of the throne of God' (Hebrews 12:2).

And that's the best good news—ever.

For further reading

GENESIS 19:15–26

The King James Version of the Bible says that Jesus 'steadfastly set his face to go to Jerusalem' (Luke 9:51). He did not flinch although he knew he was going to his death. Humanly speaking, a quiet return to the carpenter's shop in Nazareth while the fuss died down might have appeared an attractive alternative to Jesus at this point, but he was firm and resolute in his purpose, looking straight at his suffering and death and beyond that to his resurrection. There may be times when we think our old way of life was much easier and that we have given up a great deal to follow Jesus. We need to look forward, not back. We can learn a lesson from Lot's wife, who looked back to what she was leaving behind in the depraved city of Sodom and, instead of escaping, shared in its destruction. We have been rescued from our old life with its false freedoms, empty promises and lack of real satisfaction to live an abundant life now and to go to heaven when we die.

Prayer

May I run the race before me,
Strong and brave to face the foe,
Looking only unto Jesus
As I onward go.

KATIE BARCLAY WILKINSON (1859–1928)

Swallowing camels

It is for freedom that Christ has set us free. Stand firm, then, and do not let yourselves be burdened again by a yoke of slavery.

GALATIANS 5:1

I have the feeling that life is getting more complicated—and unnecessarily so. You may have seen the report from Australia revealing that the Workplace Health and Safety Office in Queensland had slammed the children's character Bob the Builder for violating their code of conduct.

In what I keep hoping was a tongue-in-cheek announcement, they pointed out that Bob breached at least seven of their safety guidelines, including driving without a seatbelt and allowing visitors on site without a helmet. He has also been spotted hanging on to the side of his bulldozer—all of which led the office to suggest that he would never be granted a licence to work in Queensland (not that I think there is any risk of his making an application).

We may smile, but this week I heard of a West Country church doing their best to serve the local community and being road-blocked along the way. Aware of changes in the law that require public buildings to be accessible to wheelchair users, they have gone to the trouble and expense of drawing up plans to install a special toilet and washroom.

You can imagine their frustration when another authority stepped in to object that the siting of the new loo didn't meet their requirements for protecting heritage buildings. So a small church finds itself caught between two government bodies, each pressing its own claims, and a good idea looks like being strangled at birth by red tape.

Jesus once used a wonderful phrase about the danger of 'straining out a gnat but swallowing a camel' (Matthew 23:24). He was challenging the hypocrisy of some religious leaders who made a fuss over little self-made rules while ignoring the really big issues. They made an art of majoring on minors, and that is not a failure limited to religious leaders.

Yes, we need rules that protect and regulations that enhance life, but when they squeeze initiative, cripple creativity and bear-hug us with bureaucracy, they have outlived their sell-by date. There are already awards for the best forms written in plain English. Another set should be launched for those who take the complex out of the complicated—and that can be achieved without dumbing down and treating us all like pre-schoolers.

I like Albert Einstein's cautionary wisdom: 'Make everything as simple as possible—but not simpler.'

For further reading

GALATIANS 5:1–16

The Christians in the churches in Galatia had heard the good news that Jesus had borne the punishment for their sins when he died on the cross, and they had put their trust in him. But then people had come among them and told them that this was not enough—they needed to be circumcised as well—so they had gone back to trying to be good enough in their own strength, by keeping rules. Paul doesn't mince words: 'You... have been alienated from Christ; you have fallen away from grace' (v. 4). There is something in human nature that wants to know what the rules are; we feel better when we know what we ought to do, and we fear having to depend on someone else. Paul makes things simple for us. We do not have to observe innumerable rules because the law can be 'summed up in a single command: "Love your neighbour as yourself"' (v. 14). And even when we fail in that, Jesus has done all that is necessary to set us free from the slavery of a sinful life and its consequences.

Prayer

Thank you, Lord Jesus, for your grace, which I have not earned and do not deserve. I want to obey you because I love you, not because I have to.

Good neighbours

So in everything, do to others what you would have them do to you.
MATTHEW 7:12

Here's a parable. A Good Samaritan was walking home one night when he saw a drunk lying on the pavement. Wanting to help, he asked, 'Do you live here?' 'Yep,' came the reply. 'Would you like me to help you upstairs?' 'Yep,' was the response.

So he carried the drunk up two flights of stairs. On reaching a doorway, the Good Samaritan panicked. What if the man's wife answered? What if she assumed they had been out drinking together? What if she blamed him for her husband's sorry state? He couldn't face a row, so the Good Samaritan gently opened the door and shoved the drunk through it.

He returned to the street but, behold, another drunk lay on the pavement before him. 'Do you live here?' he asked. 'Yep,' the man answered. 'Would you like a hand to get home?' 'Yep,' he said. Amazingly this man lived in the same block, on the same floor and in the same flat as the first one. They must be related, the Good Samaritan thought as he quietly pushed the second drunk through the door.

He returned to the street and, behold, a third drunk lay on the pavement. He bent down to offer help but the man suddenly leapt up and ran across the street to a policeman. 'Help! Help!' the drunk screamed. 'Protect me, officer. This man has been doing nothing all night but taking me upstairs and throwing me down the lift shaft!'

Like all good parables, it has a moral sting in its tale. Before you help, make sure that what you offer is what is really needed.

It is proposed to introduce 'good citizenship' classes into our schools. It's a good idea to instil a sense of responsibility in young people. In fact, the best schools already do this in a variety of ways. But as with all ideas, it poses a few difficulties. Who would want to live in a world full of busybodies minding everyone else's business but their own?

In the original parable of the good Samaritan, Jesus tells of a man who offered a wounded traveller some genuine help, with no strings attached. Far from being a mere do-gooder, the stranger in the story *did* some good and offered help where it was needed. And the parable, according to Jesus, finishes with a sting in the tail: 'Go and do likewise.'

For further reading

LUKE 10:25–37

An expert in the law had come to Jesus with a question about how he could inherit eternal life. Jesus had turned the question back to him and he had answered correctly. He could have left the matter there and both he and Jesus could be said to have come out of the encounter well, but for some reason he didn't. The Bible tells us that 'he wanted to justify himself' (v. 29). We tend to view the motives of the religious establishment in Jesus' day with some suspicion. Perhaps this expert was trying to set a trap for Jesus with his questions. On the other hand, he may genuinely have wanted to make certain he was doing enough to inherit eternal life by making sure that he had not overlooked loving someone who could be said to be his neighbour. Jesus told him the parable of the good Samaritan in reply to his question. The robbers had stripped their victim and left him unconscious. There was no way of identifying who he was or where he was from. The point is that we are not called to discern who our neighbours are; the focus is on us. Do we show ourselves to be good neighbours by our response to other people, whoever they are? Jesus' challenge to the man to 'go and do likewise' (v. 37) is to us as well.

Prayer

Ask God to show you how to 'love your neighbour as yourself' in some appropriate way today.

Don't gloat

You should not look down on your brother
in the day of his misfortune.

OBADIAH 12

I've got a question that has been bugging me. Over the past few weeks I have come across various lists of celebrities in magazines and newspapers, telling us who is 'in' at present and who is 'out'. My question is, who makes these lists up in the first place?

The other morning I read a particularly brutal version that not only told us who was a sad has-been but added some snide personal comments along the way. I think that these articles crop up at slack times when news is scarce—two or three people in the editorial office bat around their personal likes and dislikes and then compile them into an article.

This raises the fascinating issue of how and why we make judgments about other people. It also challenges us to consider if our ability to assess others is all that accurate.

There is a well-known Old Testament story of the prophet Samuel being sent on a mission to identify and anoint a new king over Israel. He is sent to a specific town and to a specific family—the household of Jesse in Bethlehem. Jesse has eight sons and Samuel has been told that one of them will be the new king. Samuel (following the traditions of his culture) assumes that the eldest son will be the chosen one, but he is stopped dead in his tracks by a message from God. 'Do not consider his appearance or his height, for I have rejected him. The Lord does not look at the things man looks at. Man looks at the outward appearance, but the Lord looks at the heart' (1 Samuel 16:7).

As the story unfolds, the youngest son, who is looking after the family's herds, is the one whom God has chosen as king—David, the smallest and most insignificant member of the family, who is not even considered important enough to be around the house to be introduced to the famous Samuel.

David was not on the 'A' list, yet turned out to be the greatest king in the history of Israel. So it seems that, as far back as 3,000 years ago, these 'celebrity assessments' were useless.

The Christian bishop Augustine reminds us of the most important assessment of all: 'God examines both rich and poor, not according to their lands and houses, but according to the riches of their hearts.'

For further reading

Obadiah 8–15; Psalm 69:19–20

When troubles come to celebrities or powerful people in the public eye, there is often an attitude promoted by the media that they have 'paid the price' for their fame, that things have been evened out between those of us who would like fortune and fame and those who have achieved it. The temptation is to join in gloating over their misfortune, especially if they have brought it on themselves. Many of those who have been turned against by the media would be able to echo the psalmist's lament: 'Scorn has broken my heart... I looked for sympathy but there was none' (v. 20). We, as God's forgiven people, should be compassionate. We know our own frailty and should not be scornful of other people's. Obadiah prophesied disaster for the people of Edom who had gloated over the destruction of the people of Israel and even assisted in it. He said, 'As you have done, it will be done to you; your deeds will return upon your own head' (v. 15). And Jesus says to us, 'In the same way as you judge others, you will be judged' (Matthew 7:2).

Prayer

Merciful God, make me compassionate, not scornful. Forgive me for the times when I have gloated over other people's misfortune.

Well-fed dustbins

Written in November 2001.

See that you also excel in this grace of giving.
2 CORINTHIANS 8:7

This week a friend passed on this thought-provoking comment from a magazine:

If you woke up this morning, you're ahead of the one million who didn't survive the week. If you can sit down, read the paper and drink a cup of coffee, you're better off than the 500 million men, women and children around the world who are currently experiencing the horrors of war, the loneliness of imprisonment, the agony of torture or the pangs of starvation.

If you can attend church without threat, you've a freedom envied by two billion others who've never been inside one. If you have food, clothes and a roof over your head, you're richer than 75 per cent of the world's inhabitants. Actually your dustbin eats better than they do.

If you have money in the bank, you are one of the world's top 8 per cent. If you own a Bible, you're better off than the 1.5 billion people who have never seen one. If you can read this, you are ahead of one-third of people on the planet who are illiterate.

Without indulging in a guilt trip, it helps to be reminded from time to time of some of the real struggles others face, and to put our own petty moans into perspective.

Last week's annual Children in Need appeal once again raised millions for good causes, and all across the south-west, people rose to the challenge with hosts of novel fund-raising ideas. Some of the stories of how the money raised last year has been used were deeply moving and a reminder of how much we take for granted.

The TV pictures of the refugee villages across Afghanistan have beamed into our homes this week, along with heart-rending stories of families in crisis. After the bombs comes the rebuilding, and the aid agencies are (as usual) rolling up their sleeves to help. I have no doubt that, through the generosity of many, millions of pounds will be raised and thousands of people saved.

Shops will be packed this weekend as the pre-Christmas build-up gathers pace. What better time to give a gift to someone you don't know out of a grateful heart.

There is a psalm that has the line, 'Praise the Lord, O my soul, and forget not all his benefits' (Psalm 103:2), and giving is always a great antidote for amnesia.

For further reading

2 CORINTHIANS 8:1–15

Despite their poverty, the Macedonian Christians had given generously, 'even beyond their ability', to meet the needs of others (v. 3). The Corinthians had started well (v. 10) but their initial enthusiasm had waned. Paul did not want to compel them to contribute. Rather, he wanted to offer them the opportunity to prove the 'sincerity of their love' (v. 8). In his previous letter, he had instructed them to put aside a proportion of their income each week which would be collected later and taken to Jerusalem to alleviate need amongst the Christians there (1 Corinthians 16:2). Paul was talking about giving that was thoughtful and planned. In the same way, we need to think and pray about how much we give to God's work, and make it a financial priority. If we cling on to the management of our finances, then we will tend to go to God only in emergencies, but if we allow God to direct our spending and giving, we will not have to worry about unexpected expense, because he knows what we need and will take care of us.

Prayer

Reflect on Jesus' words: 'Give, and it will be given to you. A good measure, pressed down, shaken together and running over, will be poured into your lap. For with the measure you use, it will be measured to you' (Luke 6:38).

Doorways to Strength

Undeserved suffering

It is commendable if a man bears up under the pain of unjust suffering because he is conscious of God.
1 PETER 2:19

For me, one of the best things about the summer holidays is the opportunity to catch up on some reading. That may seem strange as my job involves books a great deal, but I find it a change to read things outside my usual diet.

So, for example, I will read three or four of the latest fiction bestsellers and thoroughly enjoy getting lost in the fantasy world of whodunnits. This holiday I decided to add to my usual stack of paperbacks a book I have wanted to read for ages—Nelson Mandela's autobiography, *Long Walk to Freedom* (Abacus, 1995).

It is almost 800 pages long and my wife teased that I would take a fortnight to get through it. She was wrong. I couldn't put it down, and sat up for two nights until the small hours of the morning until it was finished.

It is a remarkable story about a remarkable man. If it was fiction it would be classified as brilliant, but it tells the true story of a little boy born into a small village of South Africa's Transkei, who grew up to be one of the 20th century's towering figures on the world stage. For decades his words and even his photograph could not be published in his homeland. He was imprisoned for 28 years, kept virtually isolated from the outside world.

How he rose from a prison island to the presidential palace is a story that must be read. The long struggle for justice and reconciliation in South Africa needs to be widely studied. But the part of Nelson Mandela's story that spoke most clearly to me was his ability to forgive. He stood against the evil of apartheid but seemed to have the capacity to differentiate between the system that was wrong and the people who supported it. It is the principle of 'hating the sin yet loving the sinner'.

Mandela writes of his prison experience as life-transforming: 'It was during those long and lonely years that my hunger for the freedom of my own people became a hunger for the freedom of all people, white and black. I knew as well as I knew anything that the oppressor must be liberated just as surely as the oppressed' (p. 751).

He may have been in prison but he didn't live as a prisoner. His willingness to forgive set him free long before the cell door opened.

For further reading

1 PETER 3:8–22

Undeserved suffering doesn't seem to make sense. It is far easier to accept suffering if, in some way, the sufferer appears to have brought it on himself. We feel safer if we can believe that suffering is avoidable. In this passage Peter quotes the advice of Psalm 34:12–16 on how to avoid the troubles of life—and it's good advice. If we tell lies (v. 10) and look for trouble (v. 11), we are going to find it. However, even if we are 'eager to do good', we may still 'suffer for what is right', as Nelson Mandela did. When this happens, Peter tells us, we should not be frightened, because it is a blessing (v. 14). Suffering for doing good (as opposed to getting our just punishment for doing wrong) means that we are following in the footsteps of Jesus who died for our sins, not his own. If we remain positive in troubled times, people will want to know why, and we shall then have the opportunity to tell them about Jesus (v. 15).

Prayer

For times of suffering:

'Have mercy on me, O God, have mercy! I look to you for protection. I will hide beneath the shadow of your wings until this violent storm is past' (Psalm 57:1, Living Water).

11 September 2001

Written 15 September 2001, as many churches were holding special services of remembrance

But where sin increased, grace increased all the more.
ROMANS 5:20

Tuesday 11 September 2001 is history, and for as long as history is recorded it will be a date that will be remembered. It witnessed a landmark event, the full implications of which are still unfolding.

I am reminded of some words of President John F. Kennedy: 'Only in winter can you tell which trees are truly green. Only when the winds of adversity blow can you tell whether an individual or country has steadfastness.'

This week, adversity hit hurricane force. May America prove steadfast. May we all prove steadfast.

So many words have been spoken and written over the past few days. I am struggling to absorb them and have no will to add to them. But as we look beyond ourselves for strength, I offer this prayer:

> *Almighty God,*
> *Our senses are numbed by the events of this week.*
> *Hear our prayers for those who need you at this time.*
> *For those families who grieve the loss of loved ones,*
> *For those who anxiously wait for news,*
> *For those who feel their world has ended,*
> *For those who try to bring order out of chaos,*
> *For those who offer help and healing,*
> *For those who lead and make decisions,*
> *Grant your peace.*

Lord, we pray for our world today.
Free us from evil, deliver us from prejudice and keep us from hatred.
Cause us to hunger and thirst for righteousness,
establish justice and pursue peace.
Teach us to love our neighbour as ourselves.

Father in heaven,
Have mercy on us, for in you we take refuge.
May we dwell in the shadow of your wings.
Amen.

For further reading

ROMANS 5:12–21

When Paul speaks in Romans of grace increasing where sin increased, he is talking about sin in universal terms and about the eternal life won for us by the death of Jesus. But it is often the case that God's grace to us seems to increase at times of suffering. As we heard with horror and disbelief of the evil events of 11 September 2001, we were moved by the heroism displayed by the rescue workers, the simple acts of kindness shown by ordinary people to one another, by the messages of love sent by those about to die to their families. Evil was not wholly triumphant that day. Since then, we have heard of people who have reassessed their lifestyle and their priorities and have found a renewed appreciation of what their families, friends and communities mean to them.

We have a God of immense compassion. Jesus, who was 'a man of sorrows, and familiar with suffering' (Isaiah 53:3) when he lived on earth, won a final victory against suffering, sin and death. So where sin increases, God is there, and his grace increases because evil will never have the final word.

Prayer

Almighty God, we don't understand how bad things can happen when you are all-powerful, but we do believe that you love us and we look to you for the strength to bear our sorrows in a way that honours you.

In time of deep need

Written in February 2001 during the foot-and-mouth crisis.

Yet I will rejoice in the Lord, I will be joyful in God my Saviour.
HABAKKUK 3:18

This has not been an easy week for farmers. The current outbreak of foot-and-mouth disease has led to hundreds of farms being placed under emergency restrictions and safety measures being brought into place to halt the spread of the disease.

This comes on top of a series of hard blows that the agriculture industry has faced in recent years. Reports show:

- Farm incomes have fallen by 90 per cent in the past five years.
- An average 500-acre family farm earns just £8,000 per annum.
- Prices for pigs and sheep fell so low in 1999 that thousands were killed in the fields as there was no money to feed them.
- In 2000 an estimated 23,800 farmers left the industry.

Add to this sad list the winter's devastating floods, the BSE crisis, high fuel costs and a recent outbreak of swine fever, and you begin to realize why the farming community of Britain is reeling.

Memories of 1967 have been evoked over the past few days. That was the year when foot-and-mouth last struck with force, resulting in the slaughter of thousands of animals and the isolation of farms for long months.

I was struck by a comment from a spokesman for the farmers during a radio interview yesterday. Asked what they were doing to respond to the current crisis, he said, 'We are hoping for the best, but anticipating the worst.' In other words, do all that can possibly be done to prevent the disease spreading but never give up hope that it can and will be stopped.

As it happens, 'hope' is a very Christian word. In the language of the New Testament the meaning is much stronger than our English word 'hope' suggests. It means a favourable and confident expectation based on what God has done in and through Jesus Christ. So it is not wishful thinking or misplaced optimism but a rock-solid confidence that God is as good as his word.

There are many churches in Britain who make a habit, Sunday by Sunday, of praying publicly for people and events in the news. This week the farmers and their families need our prayers, as do those who are trying to identify and control the disease, and those in authority who make decisions that affect so many lives.

Let's pray above all for the gift of hope.

For further reading

HABAKKUK 3:1–19

The book of Habakkuk consists of a conversation between the prophet and God. Habakkuk complains about the state of the nation where violence and injustice flourish and God doesn't seem to take any notice. God replies that he is going to send the Babylonians, 'a feared and dreaded people' (1:7), to conquer Israel. Habakkuk acknowledges that God is perfectly just in this, but asks how he, whose 'eyes are too pure to look on evil', can tolerate the Babylonians. Then he waits for God's answer. (Do we sometimes fail to get answers about the things that disturb us because we are not prepared to wait for them?) God responds by saying that the Babylonians will be punished in their turn. Habakkuk's prayer in chapter 3 is a wonderful outpouring of worship and confession of faith. Facing impending disaster, he declares, 'Though the fig tree does not bud and there are no grapes on the vines, though the olive crop fails and the fields produce no food, though there are no sheep in the pen and no cattle in the stalls, yet I will rejoice in the Lord, I will be joyful in God my Saviour' (3:17–18).

Prayer

'In this time of our deep need, begin again to help us, as you did in years gone by. Show us your power to save us. And in your anger, remember your mercy' (Habakkuk 3:2, Living Water).

Depression

There is a time for everything... a time to weep and a time to laugh,
a time to mourn and a time to dance.

ECCLESIASTES 3:1, 4

A man was once asked for his favourite quotation from the Bible. He chose the phrase, 'And it came to pass.' When pressed to explain such an odd choice, the man replied that he had faced many problems through his life but took great comfort from the reminder that such troubles hadn't come to stay but would eventually pass! Although I struggle to accept his interpretation of the text, I applaud the spirit that lies behind it.

I have recently read a book that deals with the difficult issue of suffering. It included the story of William Cowper, a poet and writer who lived in the 18th century.

Cowper had a long-term battle with depression when little was known about this powerful illness or how to treat it. He spent several spells in asylums and attempted suicide more than once. At the age of 32, he discovered a personal faith and found great comfort in it. He used his writing talent to express his new-found faith in Christ, and a number of his hymns have become classics in the English-speaking world.

But although his faith was a strength to him, it didn't remove the long bouts of depression that returned on a cyclical basis. He was grateful for close friends, including his vicar, the famous John Newton, who stood by him in those dark days.

Cowper's story reminds us that faith is not a passport to a trouble-free life but it does offer strength beyond our own limited resources.

Perhaps Cowper's best-known hymn is 'God moves in a mysterious way'. The words are even more enriching when you recognize that they were crafted by someone who knew the truth of which he wrote:

God moves in a mysterious way his wonders to perform
He plants his footsteps in the sea, and rides upon the storm.

Judge not the Lord by feeble sense, but trust him for his grace,
Behind a frowning providence he hides a smiling face.

His purposes will ripen fast, unfolding every hour;
The bud may have a bitter taste, but sweet will be the flower.

Ye fearful saints, fresh courage take, the clouds ye so much dread
Are big with mercy and shall break in blessings on your head.

For further reading

PSALM 13:1–6

Depression can be very lonely, because nobody else can know exactly how you feel or what it is like to be you. Most people experience a degree of depression at some time in their lives. If it is in response to sad events or pressures, then it is much easier to understand, for you and for other people. If it comes out of the blue with no obvious external cause, as it did for William Cowper, it is much more frightening. In such times, we may not feel like it but God is right there. He, only he, truly understands. Sometimes all you can do is wait for the dark time to pass. All your efforts to 'pull yourself together', to try different ways of getting to feel better, are unavailing. God does not blame you for that. He loves you just as much when you are incapable of praying as when you spend hours in prayer. His love never fails. He will not let you go.

Prayer

Thank you, Lord, that you are with me in the tough times. I know this, even though I don't always feel it. 'I trust in your unfailing love' (Psalm 13:5).

Greater love

Written in August 2000. James Mawdsley was freed fom prison to work and campaign against injustice.

And everyone who has left houses or brothers or sisters or father or mother or children or fields for my sake will receive a hundred times as much and will inherit eternal life.

MATTHEW 19:29

I don't know what you've planned for the Bank Holiday weekend, but there's one young man who won't be enjoying a break.

James Mawdsley faces another long day in a small cell with just one 20-minute period for exercise and no human company except for those who guard him. Next week is the first anniversary of his arrest and he will be in jail for quite a few more. He has been sentenced to 17 years.

If you don't know James' story, let me fill in some details. He is 27 years old, tall, good-looking, and those who know him describe him as a thoroughly nice guy. He is very bright (five straight As at A' level) and studied at Bristol University. Like many students, he opted for a gap year and travelled to Australia.

While there he met some Burmese refugees who told horrific stories of the brutal military regime in their homeland. James decided to travel home via Burma. He arrived there in 1997 and taught English for a time. What he saw confirmed all he had heard. He witnessed first-hand the injustice and cruelty, and he decided in his heart to do something.

He made a couple of peaceful public protests and was arrested and deported. Then last August he returned to Burma and handed out leaflets which made no more radical comments than urging the government to reopen the universities and encouraging people to oppose unjust laws. The military were incensed and he was arrested and sentenced.

James' family is standing with him. Distinguished politicians such as

Lord Alton and Baroness Cox have taken up his case and the leading QC, Lord Brennan, recently travelled to Mandalay to handle his appeal. The UN Commission on Human Rights has sent a full report to the Burmese Government demanding his release. In June, eighteen Congressmen and five Senators signed a letter of support.

To many Burmese people, James is a hero. He is a devout Christian who sees his identification with them as an outworking of his faith. He cares deeply that so many have been tortured, raped and killed. It matters to him that the party democratically elected ten years ago cannot hold office and its Premier is under arrest.

James Mawdsley cared enough to get involved—the parable of the good Samaritan in 21st-century clothes. Only this is no parable.

For further reading

HEBREWS 11:24–26; JOHN 15:9–17

When Jesus said, 'Greater love has no one than this, that he lay down his life for his friends' (John 15:13), he was talking to his disciples about the death he himself had come to die for their sake and ours, and at the same time he was calling them and us to follow his example. Moses could have carried on living in luxury in Egypt. Instead he chose to be identified with the Egyptians' Israelite slaves (Hebrews 11:25). James Mawdsley laid aside the prospect of a much easier way of life and identified himself with the Burmese people, suffering with them. We too are called to lay down our lives in service to God. That does not necessarily mean that we have to die, but we do have to put to one side our desire to be comfortable and seek to serve God in serving others, however costly that may be. In this way we will bear 'fruit that will last' (John 15:16) and receive a reward from God (Hebrews 11:26).

Prayer

Lord Jesus, please show me how you want me to serve others for your sake, and grant me the strength to do it.

The ultimate statistic

Death is the destiny of every man; the living should take this to heart.
ECCLESIASTES 7:2

Do you know what George Bernard Shaw described as the 'ultimate statistic'? The answer is 'death' because, as Shaw pointed out, we know that one out of one person dies.

Now there's a happy subject for a weekend read, I hear you say, so let me explain.

I am preaching tomorrow at a neighbouring church. They contacted me with details of the service and gave a title for my sermon. They are running a teaching series on important issues in life such as getting married, building friendships, handling money and so on. My subject is the final one, they told me, and the title is 'How to face death'.

That explains why, for the past few days, I have been doing some serious thinking on the subject. Two quotations have stopped me in my tracks, both from people who became world figures and recipients of the prestigious Nobel Peace Prize.

The first is from Dag Hammarskjold, former Secretary General of the United Nations, who wrote, 'In the last analysis it is our conception of death which decides the answers to all the questions life puts to us.' Whoever heard of a bunch of ramblers struggling to find a route on a map when none of them had a final destination in mind?

The second comes from Dr Martin Luther King, who faced the heart-rending task of conducting a funeral service for a group of children who were murdered in 1961. The children had been attending Sunday School when a bomb planted by a racist group exploded.

Part of his funeral sermon contained these remarkable faith-filled words:

I hope you can find some consolation from Christianity's affirmation that death is not the end. Death is not a [full stop] that ends the great sentence of life but a comma that punctuates it to a more lofty significance. Death is not a blind alley that leads the human race into a state of nothingness but an open door which leads man to life eternal. May this daring faith, this great invincible surmise, be your sustaining power during these trying days.

It has been said that (looking at Western society) never in the history of the human race have people had so much to live with, yet so little to live for. But the empty cross and the empty grave of Jesus offer daring faith and living hope.

For further reading

2 KINGS 4:8–37

The Bible does not explain why the Shunammite woman exercised such generous hospitality towards Elisha, but perhaps she felt that having this man of God staying at her house would protect her and be a source of blessing. God showed his power to her when she gave birth to a son after she had given up hope of ever having children. Understandably, when he died she suffered 'bitter distress' (v. 27) that God appeared to have given with one hand and taken back with the other. She demonstrated her faith by going to God's man, Elisha, for answers and God restored her son to her in response to the prophet's prayer. Tragedy is no respecter of persons. Being a Christian does not guarantee immunity from pain. Suffering may test our faith in a loving God, especially when we are personally affected, but we show the quality of our faith when we turn to him for comfort and help.

Prayer

I will trust in you at all times and pour out my heart to you, for you are my refuge, O God (based on Psalm 62:8).

Can God heal the pain?

Written in March 1996 during the Making Waves mission in Plymouth.

He heals the brokenhearted and binds up their wounds.
PSALM 147:3

If you were born with a cleft palate, misshapen lips, a crooked nose, lop-sided teeth and garbled speech, you could be forgiven for feeling self-conscious. Mary Ann Bird knows how it feels, and grew up believing that no one outside her family could love her. She told other children she was injured in a dreadful accident rather than admit she had been born deformed.

One person stood out in her childhood—a much-loved school teacher called Mrs Leonard, a round, happy, sparkling lady. Mary recalls an incident that healed her damaged self-image:

Annually we had a hearing test. Mrs Leonard gave the test to everyone in the class and finally it was my turn. I knew from past years that, as we stood against the door and covered one ear, the teacher sitting at her desk would whisper something and we would repeat it back, things like 'The sky is blue' or 'Do you have new shoes?' I waited for those words that God must have put into her mouth, those seven words that changed my life. Mrs Leonard said in her whisper, 'I wish you were my little girl.'

Words can hurt and heal. Mary Ann Bird heard the healing sort and they transformed her.

This week the Plymouth Pavilions hosts a unique programme entitled 'Get a Life!' Supported by churches in the region, its aim is to explain and explore what real faith can offer in what sometimes appears to be a meaningless world. Mime, music, dance and face-to-face interviews with media celebrities and with local people will be blended together in a fast-moving programme. One of the country's most respected Christian communicators, Dr Donald English, will take an honest look at Jesus—who he is, why he came and why he matters today.

They are following a well-trodden path. One of the first Christian leaders, Paul, wrote of his work, 'I have become all things to all men, so that by all possible means I might save some' (1 Corinthians 9:22). The message cannot be changed but the clothes it dresses in must, if the church is to be on the cutting edge.

God places no limitations on how and when he speaks. Thankfully, he has never been confined to church services at 11.00am and 6.30pm. In a classroom or a theatre, God is still in the business of bringing words that help and heal.

For further reading

JOB 3:1–26

Many of us suffer emotional pain due to some disadvantage in our life or events in our past, and for some people that pain seems never-ending. When God brings healing of this kind of pain, he rarely does it as a single act, making our problems and sadness disappear all at once. Usually he works in a variety of ways, gradually bringing us to wholeness and peace, but we can be certain that God is always with us, even at our darkest times. In fact, in all of our past life's circumstances he was there at the time and he cared, even though we may not have known him then or been aware of his presence. Just as God does not leave us alone, he sometimes sends others, like Mrs Leonard, with the right words at the right time to help and heal. Though it may take a long time, we can cling to this promise in Psalm 147: 'He heals the brokenhearted and binds up their wounds'.

Prayer

O Lord, you alone can heal me; you alone can save. My praises are for you alone (Jeremiah 17:14, Living Water).

Doorways to the Church Year

Missing out

Mary has chosen what is better, and it will not be taken away from her.
LUKE 10:42

It was the busy build-up to Christmas in a smart Californian suburb. The last thing one particular household needed was a bunch of bright, happy carol singers. The singers approached the front door and cleared their throats, ready to oblige the family with any favourite request. The lady of the house opened the door and let them have it with both barrels.

She was *very* busy, the plumbing was on the blink and no one could find a plumber to fix it. She had a crowd expected for dinner any minute, and no, she didn't have any special request other than, 'Go away and come back another time!'

'Yes, ma'am. Sorry to have troubled you,' replied the group leader— and Bing Crosby dutifully moved his volunteer choir further down the street.

Sadly, we sometimes miss out on really good things because our lives are cluttered with not-so-important things.

The start of a new year is often seized as a chance to change, to take stock and shift direction, to clear out some of the not-so-important things and to concentrate on what really matters. But for changes to work, two things are crucial—first, a clear sense of purpose; and second, a power beyond ourselves.

I recently came across a poem from the pen of Thomas Dekker, the 17th-century dramatist. It is simply entitled 'My Purpose'.

> To awaken each morning with a smile brightening my face;
> To greet each day with reverence for the opportunities it contains;
> To approach my work with a clean mind;
> To hold ever before me, even in the doing of little things,

> *the Ultimate Purpose toward which I am working;*
> *To meet men and women with laughter on my lips and love in my heart;*
> *To be gentle, kind and courteous through all the hours;*
> *To approach the night with weariness that ever woos sleep,*
> *and the joy that comes from work well done—*
> *This is how I desire to waste wisely my days.*

I hope that this new year goes well for you and yours, but most of all, that the changes you face may all be for the better.

For further reading

LUKE 10:38–42

Have you ever wished you were alive during Jesus' earthly life and had the opportunity to meet him? Martha was and did. She was a hospitable woman who invited Jesus and his disciples into her home. She wanted everything to be perfect and threw herself into her preparations. Most of us have, at one time or another, experienced the frustration of feeling that we have been left to do all the work while other people sit around enjoying themselves, so we can imagine how Martha became crosser and crosser and more and more sorry for herself when it didn't seem to occur to Mary to come and give her a hand. Even Jesus didn't seem to notice how busy she was. Finally she exploded at him, 'Don't you care?' In her preoccupation with making a good impression, she had missed out on hearing what Jesus had to say, and her temper had let her down in front of him. She had an opportunity many of us would envy, and she wasted it.

Prayer

Lord, keep me spiritually aware so that I won't miss out on the truly good things in life in the midst of earthly cares.

He stoops to conquer

And being found in appearance as a man, he humbled himself and became obedient to death—even death on a cross!

PHILIPPIANS 2:8

Watching the Oscars ceremony the other evening, I was reminded of the words of the late Marilyn Monroe: 'Hollywood is a place where they'll pay you a thousand dollars for a kiss and fifty cents for your soul.'

I happen to like cinema as an art form, but the plastic hype and shallow *bonhomie* I can live without. No matter how hard they try, the film fraternity just look plain stupid each year at Oscar time.

During Lent, it's helpful to consider different aspects of the character of Jesus as portrayed in the Gospels. Today, in stark contrast to Hollywood, I want to focus on his humility.

The New Testament speaks of Jesus humbling himself, or making himself of no reputation. This attitude is seen at its climax by his willingness to go to the cross. To the Jewish mind, it was the worst death a man could die, as it symbolized being cursed by God. To the Gentile, it was a death fit only for a slave or a rebel, the lowest of the low.

Why such humility? As the great Christian thinker, Athanasius, put it: 'He became what we are, that he might make us what he is.'

There is a Jewish joke about a rabbi, a cantor and the synagogue cleaner preparing for the Day of Atonement. The rabbi prays and beats his breast, saying, 'I am nothing, I am nothing.' The cantor, following his lead, does the same and prays, 'I am nothing, I am nothing.' It's the cleaner's turn and he bows his head, beats his breast and murmurs, 'I am nothing, I am nothing.' At this the rabbi turns to the cantor and whispers in disgust, 'Look who thinks he's nothing!'

There is nothing false about the humility of Jesus Christ. In his own words: 'The Son of Man did not come to be served but to serve and to give his life as a ransom for many' (Matthew 20:28). Here are no expensive costumes, gushing speeches and elaborate stage sets, but a naked man, a howling mob and a Roman scaffold. And no gold statuette as a memento for the mantelpiece, simply the accolade of a multitude of free and forgiven people.

The New Testament says that he was rich but became poor, so that through his poverty we might become rich. Truly, he is the king who stoops to conquer.

For further reading

1 SAMUEL 20:12–17, 24–34

Jonathan was the son of King Saul and could, not unnaturally, have expected to succeed his father one day. He was a godly, valiant man (1 Samuel 14:12–14), who inspired loyalty and admiration (14:45). There was every reason to think that he would have made a good king but Jonathan acknowledged that David would be king, not him— 'May the Lord be with you as he has been with my father' (20:13)—and asked that David would protect him rather than establishing his rule by murdering any other possible claimants to the throne (20:14). The key to Jonathan's willingness to humble himself and be David's subject rather than his ruler is found in verse 17: Jonathan 'loved him as he loved himself'. Jesus humbled himself, becoming a man and dying a terrible death out of love for us. We show our love for him and for others when we are willing to forget about our 'rights' and be a servant of others.

Prayer

Lord, you said that anyone who wants to be great in your kingdom must be a servant of others (Mark 10:43). Forgive my pride and my desire to look good to other people and help me to be more like Jesus.

It's not too late

Father, forgive them, for they do not know what they are doing.
LUKE 23:34

As anyone from Yorkshire will tell you, 'There's now't so queer as folk.' And there's none so fickle either. As you may well have discovered to your cost, people can love you one minute and leave you the next.

Within the unfolding story of the Easter event, Palm Sunday stands as a noisy witness to human inconsistency. A large crowd gathered to welcome Jesus into the city for the most important religious festival of the year. They were speculating as to what this so-called miracle worker would say or do, and many wanted a closer look. Then crowd fever gripped them. They spread their clothes, waved palm branches and shouted their slogans. Matthew records the after-shock: 'When Jesus entered Jerusalem, the whole city was stirred and asked, "Who is this?"' (Matthew 21:10).

But in a matter of days, public opinion turned—or had been turned, for spin-doctoring is not a modern profession. The crowd changed their theme song from 'Hosanna' to 'Crucify' without even stopping to notice their inconsistency. Not everyone followed the fickle crowd: some recognized that Jesus was extraordinary and a few had accepted him as God's Messiah. But for the majority, by Good Friday he was yesterday's news.

In case we feel judgmental, we are reminded that indifference is as great a sin. G.A. Studdert Kennedy wrote a famous poem entitled 'Indifference', which has the following verse:

> *When Jesus came to Birmingham, they simply passed Him by,*
> *They never hurt a hair of Him, they only let Him die,*
> *For men had grown more tender, and they would not give Him pain,*
> *They only just passed down the street, and left Him in the rain.*

And here lies a mystery. When Jesus was crucified, he prayed a heartfelt prayer: 'Father, forgive them, for they do not know what they are doing.'

It was a prayer for the callous soldiers who hammered the nails, the cynical crowd who changed their minds, the hypocritical religious leaders who plotted his death, the betraying Judas who sold a friend for cash and the cowardly disciples who protected their own skins. Oh yes, and for callous, indifferent people who, with impeccable niceness, simply close the door in his face with a 'Not today, thank you.'

Now that is love.

For further reading

LUKE 23:32–49

The accounts of Jesus' death on the cross differ slightly in each of the four Gospels, possibly suggesting that they describe the scene at different stages during that day. Matthew and Mark describe how the men crucified with Jesus taunted him, but at some point, perhaps impressed by Jesus' lack of retaliation and his forgiveness of his tormentors, one of them rebuked the other and asked Jesus, 'Remember me when you come into your kingdom' (Luke 23:40–42). The soldiers who had beaten Jesus and gambled for his clothes saw the events accompanying his death and were 'terrified' (Matthew 27:54), convinced that he was 'the Son of God'. Even the crowd who had mocked him earlier went away beating their breasts. No one was unaffected. Perhaps the seeds sown by the events of Good Friday bore fruit on the day of Pentecost when so many responded to Peter's preaching (Acts 2:41). It wasn't too late for them to change their minds. It is not yet too late for any of us.

Prayer

Thank you, Father, for the death of Jesus that paid the price, once and for all, for our sins. Thank you, too, for his resurrection, which promises that death need not be the end for us.

Waiting hopefully

Come… let us walk in the light of the Lord.
ISAIAH 2:5

Saturday is a strange day in the Easter festival because in many churches it's a day without a name.

We have Maundy Thursday and its association with the Last Supper and the betrayal and arrest of Jesus. We have Good Friday and the commemoration of his trial and execution. Then there is Sunday, Easter Day, that celebrates the remarkable facts of an empty tomb, folded grave clothes, the risen Jesus meeting his astonished disciples.

But what of the Saturday in between? It has no special title because nothing important took place—or so it seems.

The body of Jesus lay cold in the sealed tomb, surrounded by guards posted to deter the man's followers from stealing the corpse. That was the last thing on their mind, though. They were keeping a low profile behind locked doors, shaken with terror at the events of the past few hours and living in fear of the same fate overtaking them.

We know the end of the story, so it is difficult to understand what a dark time this must have been for those who had given up everything to follow Jesus, only to find their cherished dreams lying in a ruined mess. Saturday was the day the shock began to take hold—the bottom of the pit; the lowest point.

The writer Philip Yancey has helped me to understand the significance of Easter Saturday. More than that, he has helped me to see how it fits into the here-and-now experience of faith. He points out that those who follow Jesus today live, in a cosmic scale, on Easter Saturday—waiting for the total fulfilment of his resurrection promise to us.

Is it possible for God to bring something good out of the traumas we have witnessed around the world—the pain of Mozambique and Angola, the injustice of Zimbabwe and Bosnia, and the bleak sadness of so many lives? Easter Sunday says 'yes' with certainty. Easter Saturday says 'yes' by faith. It is in that sense that we live between promise and fulfilment.

In Yancey's words, from his book *What's So Amazing About Grace* (Zondervan, 2000):

It is a good thing to remember that in the cosmic drama, we live out our days on Saturday, the in-between day with no name. I know a woman whose grandmother lies under 150-year-old live oak trees in the cemetery of an Episcopal church in rural Louisiana. In accordance with the grandmother's instructions, only one word is carved on the tombstone: 'Waiting.'

So I would like to wish you a very happy Easter Saturday: the day that waits—with hope.

For further reading

ISAIAH 2:1–11

This is a beautiful prophecy by Isaiah, of a time when God will be given his rightful place and wars will cease and peace prevail. Verse 6 therefore comes as a shock when it reads, 'You have abandoned your people' and goes on to describe what the people of Israel would face as a result of turning away from God. Suffering is the experience of so many today. The sorrows of the world overwhelm us. We feel powerless and hopeless as peace initiatives fail and violence escalates. There are those who have grown up never knowing anything but war and poverty in their homelands. It is hard for us to imagine a time when 'nation will not take up sword against nation, nor will they train for war any more' (v. 4), but we can trust in God's promise that this time will come. And while we wait and hope, we can pray for peacemakers and aid workers, that they will continue to work to make a difference and not be discouraged, and for leaders and governments that they will seek peaceful ways of resolving their differences.

Prayer

Ask God to show you the part you should play in giving, or even in going, to help those who are more needy than you.

Resurrection power

Written in April 1998 at the time of the signing of what became known as the Good Friday Agreement. Many Christians prefer to call it the Belfast Agreement, as there was only one 'Good Friday Agreement' made once for all, 2000 years ago.

By his power God raised the Lord from the dead, and he will raise us also.

1 CORINTHIANS 6:14

Two days ago I stood in two minutes' silence. The occasion was not a funeral but a training event, and those present were invited to stand silently and pray for the Northern Ireland peace talks. For almost thirty years I have heard prayers for peace in Northern Ireland but here there were no words, simply the sound of silence.

Time will tell how significant this weekend's agreement will be in the overall story of Ireland. There are cynics and others still intent on bloodshed but, for men and women of goodwill, this political settlement offers a better chance of lasting peace than anything else in recent history.

It is significant that these events take place at the same time that Christians the world over are remembering the death and resurrection of Jesus Christ. It is wrong to suggest that the problems in Ireland stem from a war between Protestants and Catholics. The issues that divide the country go much deeper. But undoubtedly, religious belief plays a part in constructing the cultural outlook of both sides.

It is worth remembering that Christ died for all. That includes religious as well as irreligious people, black and white, slave and free, Protestants as well as Catholics. The New Testament speaks graphically of the cross of Christ having the power to destroy the barriers and dividing walls that people erect (Ephesians 2:14).

Easter Day reminds us of the power of God in raising Christ to life.

From death, darkness and despair, Jesus rose again. The same power that brought him to life is able to transform the most hopeless situations.

The access point to the forgiveness of Good Friday and the resurrection power of Easter Sunday is contained in one word—faith. That means more than belief alone. It involves laying your whole weight on that belief. It is belief with action.

Let us hope and pray that Easter 1998 will mark a turning point in Northern Ireland and that the reality of Christ's death and resurrection would turn belief into action on both sides of the divide.

In the words of Martin Luther King's prayer: 'And now to him who is able to keep us from falling, and to lift us from the dark valley of despair to the bright mountain of hope, from the midnight of desperation to the daybreak of joy. To him be power and authority for ever and ever. Amen.'

For further reading

MATTHEW 24:3–35

We thank God when peace comes to war-torn parts of the world, but we will not see a final end to war and conflict until Jesus returns at the end of time. He himself said that we should not be 'alarmed' when we 'hear of wars and rumours of wars' (v. 6). This does not mean that God has given up on the world or that he is powerless to intervene. We do not understand why 'such things *must* happen' but we should not despair. Rather we should be encouraged that man-made and natural disasters are 'the beginning of birth pains' which herald the return of Jesus. Peace does not come easily in earthly conflicts. Our peace with God was not won without pain; we can only begin to imagine what Jesus suffered as he died on the cross for us. His resurrection power to change hearts and lives brings us hope in the dark times of this life and it is our powerful security for the life to come.

Prayer

Call to mind various conflicts going on at this time in the world. Pray that God will cause the desire for peace to increase and to overwhelm hatred and the desire for revenge.

The one who falls down beside us

Written in June 2000.

Do not put out the Spirit's fire... Hold on to the good.

1 THESSALONIANS 5:19, 21

All over the weekend, Christians will be celebrating a special anniversary. Sunday marks the day known as Pentecost or Whitsun. It commemorates the coming of the Holy Spririt following Jesus' ascension to heaven. It is sometimes referred to as the birthday of the Church because of the dramatic change that took place in the outlook and priorities of the first disciples.

This millennium year is the 2,000th birthday so it is hardly surprising that there will be a few parties this weekend.

That raises the question, who is the Holy Spirit and what does he do?

Putting it simply, he is part of the Trinity—Father, Son and Spirit. He is personal, not a force or an 'it', and carries out God's work in the world. He convicts, convinces and converts, bringing people into a relationship with God through faith in Christ. He helps us to pray, guides and directs us, brings courage, healing, gifts and power. In short, no Holy Spirit equals no faith. He is indispensable.

Jesus' parting words before his ascension spoke of the Spirit: 'You will receive power when the Holy Spirit comes on you and you will be my witnesses in Jerusalem, and in all Judea and Samaria and to the ends of the earth' (Acts 1:8). The worldwide celebrations this weekend confirm the prophetic accuracy of his words.

One word used in the Bible to describe the Holy Spirit is 'Paraclete' and the various English words used to translate it reveal the difficulty of capturing its full meaning in a single word. 'Comforter', 'advocate', 'helper' and 'friend' all convey the sense of one called alongside to give us help.

A rich example came from some Bible translators working with a tribe in equatorial Africa. They struggled to find a way to translate 'Paraclete' in a dynamically equivalent word or phrase. Then they noticed that whenever the tribe travelled, the team of heavily laden porters had a spare man who carried nothing. They asked why and were told that he was there in case anyone became tired or injured. His job was to carry their load and ensure that the team was covered. They even had a name for this valuable job: 'the one who falls down beside us'.

The translators had their word—and on this special Pentecost anniversary we have a picture of who the Spirit is, why he came and what he can do.

For further reading

1 THESSALONIANS 5:16–22; EPHESIANS 4:29–32

When we first become Christians the Holy Spirit comes to live in our hearts, first showing us our sinfulness and our need of a Saviour, then giving us the assurance that we are truly saved. But the presence of the Spirit is not just something we know internally. He also manifests himself outwardly in the gifts that he gives for the building up of God's people. Therefore we need to be very careful that we 'do not put out the Spirit's fire', as Paul expresses it (1 Thessalonians 5:19), particularly with regard to prophecy (that is, the speaking out of God's truth). It is wrong to 'treat prophecies with contempt' (v. 20), because they come from God and not from men. This does not mean that if someone claims to be speaking words from God we should accept them unquestioningly. We are to 'test everything' so that we can 'hold on to the good' and 'avoid... evil' (vv. 21–22). We must be careful not to grieve the Holy Spirit either (Ephesians 4:30). Verse 31 describes the kind of behaviour that will do this and verse 32 tells us how we should behave instead.

Prayer

Holy Spirit, work through me to build up other Christians and to draw to Jesus those who do not yet know you.

What's in a name?

The seventy-two returned with joy and said, 'Lord, even the demons submit to us in your name.'
LUKE 10:17

I've done it four times and avoided offending anyone in the process. They were big decisions to make. After all, the name you give your child will stick with them for life unless they choose to change it. Every now and then you hear of a couple naming their child after the entire first team of their favourite football club, so you can hardly blame some kids for correcting the stupidity of their parents.

Fortunately my four sons tell me they are happy with their names, so at least my wife and I have done one thing right.

When it comes to naming children there are fads and fashions. This year's Elvis and Cleo give way to Tarquin and Estelle and so on it goes.

Some centuries back, the Puritans were heavily into religious-sounding names, so calling your child for lunch was rather like preaching a sermon. One family that boasted the surname Barebone named their three sons Praise God, Christ-came-into-the-world-to-save, and If-Christ-had-not-died-thou-hast-been-damned. Hearing the register called in their school must have been entertaining.

Preachers from the same period had intimidating names. I read of some Sussex ministers called Fight-the-good-fight-of-faith White, Safety-on-high Snat and Fly-fornication Richardson. I just hope they never appeared on the same bill.

When it came to Mary and Joseph and an unexpected pregnancy, some practical details were taken out of their hands, including the naming of their child. According to Dr Luke's account, the angel who announced that Mary would carry God's Son in her womb also told the astonished teenager, 'You are to give him the name Jesus' (Luke 1:31).

Jesus (or Joshua in the Hebrew version) was a fairly common name at that time. It means simply 'the Lord saves' and Matthew, in his report on this extraordinary event, adds the reason behind the choice of the name, 'You are to give him the name Jesus, because he will save his people from their sins' (Matthew 1:21).

So the name of the baby whose birth is celebrated across the globe every December sets out his credentials, his mission and his relevance to every generation. By his birth, death and resurrection, God can be known. The light shone, and still shines his restless illuminating power 2000 years on.

What's in a name? Everything when it comes to Jesus.

For further reading

LUKE 10:17–24

Jesus had sent out 72 of his disciples to prepare the way for his ministry. They came back to him, full of excitement, because they had experienced the power of his name to make even the demons submit. Jesus' name gave them authority and protection against Satan and his evil works (v. 19), but Jesus did not want them to get so hung up on the power of his name that they missed the real reason to get excited. He told them to 'rejoice that your names are written in heaven' (v. 20). Revelation 3:5 says, 'He who overcomes will… be dressed in white. I will never blot out his name from the book of life, but will acknowledge his name before my Father and his angels.' Whether your parents saddled you with an embarrassing name or one that you're proud to have, it doesn't really matter. What matters is not the power wielded in this life but the place we will occupy for eternity.

Prayer

Whether you feel you occupy an important position in the world or a very insignificant one, thank Jesus that he knows your name and that one day he will acknowledge you in heaven.

Doorways to Wisdom

Not guilty

If we claim to be without sin, we deceive ourselves and the truth is not in us.

1 JOHN 1:8

Whatever happened to guilt? I ask because the question cropped up in a conversation this morning. My publisher congratulated me on completing a job ahead of a deadline and I made a light-hearted comment that a sense of guilt always sharpens my focus for getting jobs done. She responded with a laugh and said, 'I guess we all need a bit of guilt to get us going!'

Please don't get me wrong. I know some close friends who struggle under a weight of guilt that has crippled them emotionally, and I have met others whose lives are miserable through carrying an overload of the stuff.

Perhaps the kind of guilt I mean would be better described as a sense of personal responsibility, coupled with a feeling of letting others down when you fail to achieve your goal.

Two well-known personalities have hit the nail on the head in addressing this issue recently. Broadcaster and journalist John Humphrys has written a thought-provoking book, entitled *Devil's Advocate* (Hutchinson, 2000), which provides a social commentary on contemporary Britain. It's not a pretty picture. He offers a stunningly accurate analysis, including a chapter entitled 'The Victim Culture' that pinpoints the modern fashion for finding someone else to blame. Here's a taster: 'Seeing ourselves as victims means we stop seeing ourselves as responsible.' In other words, whatever goes wrong, it's someone else's fault, never mine.

The second writer is Ben Elton in his best-selling book (and a successful play) *Popcorn* (Pocket Books, 1997). One of the characters vents his fury at the way in which people studiously avoid taking responsibility for their actions:

Nothing is anybody's fault. We don't do wrong, we have problems. We're victims, alcoholics, sexaholics. Do you know you can be a shopaholic? That's right, people aren't greedy anymore, oh no. They're shopaholics, victims of commercialism. Victims! People don't fail anymore. They experience negative success. We're building a culture of gutless, spineless, self-righteous, whining cry-babies who have an excuse for everything and take responsibility for nothing.

Now if those two quotes had come in a sermon from a bishop, we'd probably stifle a yawn, nod in agreement and think nothing more of it. But coming from the pens of a distinguished journalist and a leading comedy writer who, it would seem, have no religious axes to grind, those two comments lay down a marker—and it's a marker well worth considering.

For further reading

ROMANS 3:19–31

Guilt is a good thing some of the time. When Peter preached his first sermon in Jerusalem, his Jewish listeners were 'cut to the heart' (Acts 2:37) because of their part in crucifying the Messiah. By acknowledging their guilt, they were ready to receive God's forgiveness and new life in him. If we are followers of Jesus, then there has been a time in our lives when we recognized that we had fallen short of God's glory (Romans 3:23) and needed his intervention to deal with our sinfulness. Some of us come to this point at a time we can pinpoint; for others it is a gradual process that we recognize as we look back on it; but for none of us does it mean that we will never again let God down. God does not want us to get mired down in our guilty feelings but to come to him, believing the promise that 'if we confess our sins, he is faithful and just and will forgive us our sins and purify us from all unrighteousness' (1 John 1:9).

Prayer

Sing, O sing of my Redeemer!
With his blood he purchased me,
On the cross he sealed my pardon,
Paid the debt and set me free.

PHILIP PAUL BLISS (1838–76)

Making an impression

The man who looks intently into the perfect law that gives freedom, and continues to do this, not forgetting what he has heard, but doing it—he will be blessed in what he does.

JAMES 1:25

Imagine being on board a packed plane with one very drunk and abusive passenger. It happened to Billy Graham once. A fellow traveller became incensed when the cabin crew refused to serve him any more alcohol. They tried to pacify him but he became louder and more profane in his language. Eventually, an attendant pointed out that the famous evangelist was sitting a few rows in front, perhaps hoping that this would make the man moderate his behaviour.

Instead, the passenger stumbled to his feet shouting, 'Billy Graham! Where is he? I want to talk to him.' Her peace initiative in ruins, the crew member tried to stop him but the passenger brushed her aside and lurched unsteadily down the aisle. He stopped at the evangelist's seat and, with a menacing gaze, slurred, 'Are you really Billy Graham?' The nervous preacher quietly acknowledged that this was his name. The man's face broke into a beaming smile as he made a sudden grab. 'Then I want to shake your hand. Your sermons have been a big influence on my life!'

With testimonials like that, who needs publicity?

I heard Billy Graham repeat the story of this awkward incident, and he followed it up with a penetrating point. It's one thing to hear the truth and quite another to put it into practice.

One of the most practical, down-to-earth writings in the Bible is a letter written by a Christian leader called James. He warns of the danger of listening but not doing:

Remember, it is a message to obey, not just to listen to. So don't fool yourselves. For if a person just listens and doesn't obey, he is like a man looking at his face in a mirror. As soon as he walks away, he can't see himself any more or remember what he looks like. But if anyone keeps looking steadily into God's law for free men, he will not only remember it but he will do what it says, and God will greatly bless him in everything he does.

JAMES 1:22–25 (LIVING BIBLE)

Churchill wrote, 'Men occasionally stumble over the truth, but most of them pick themselves up and hurry off as if nothing had happened.'

According to the latest figures, over five million of us will be in churches and chapels across the UK this weekend. And here's the challenge: will the truth set us free or simply tickle our ears for a few minutes?

For further reading

JUDGES 16:23–31

Samson was a man who made a big impression. His birth was heralded by an angel and he was brought up to know that he was different from other people. The outward sign of his special calling from God was long hair that had never been cut, and the manifestation of God's power in his life was his incredible strength. However, he had one weakness— women. When he became involved with Delilah, Samson met his match. Perhaps he was so used to his unusual strength that he had become arrogant, forgetting that it depended on God. Delilah's nagging wore him down until he put himself in her power and she delivered him up to his enemies. When the Philistines brought the blinded Samson out to entertain them, perhaps for the first time he consciously depended on God and was given back his phenomenal strength for one last act. Samson did not remember God until it was too late for him. We, however, should take James' warning to heart and and be obedient listeners to God. Then we will be blessed in what we do (James 1:25).

Prayer

I want to be a doer, not just a listener. Help me to remember what you say to me and to do it, Lord.

Big Brother

Written during the first series of Big Brother in August 2000.

If you think you are standing firm, be careful that you don't fall!
1 CORINTHIANS 10:12

There have been major questions this week. Should Nick have left the house? Did his behaviour merit being banned? Is he a genuine participant or an actor planted to spice up the programme?

For those who haven't a clue what I am talking about—congratulations, you are truly sane, and long may your sanity continue. Others will know that I'm referring to the Channel 4 programme *Big Brother*, which this week saw an unexpected turn of events.

It is a game show with a difference. Ten contestants are holed up in a house for several weeks with every move covered by TV cameras. Each week, players and viewers vote to have one person removed. The last one left standing wins £70,000 and a place in the tacky TV record books.

Nick is a contestant who has not behaved well, to put it mildly, and has created an outcry. Nasty Nick, as he has been dubbed, has been accused of making up stories about his past, plotting against his fellow contestants and being two-faced. This week his pigeons came home to roost and his double-dealings were exposed. The only option was for the programme makers to remove Nick from the house or face a revolt from the other contestants.

The papers have been full of comments, most quite sniffy, about this new 'low' in entertainment. One likened it to gladiators fighting in Roman arenas to keep the crowds amused. My favourite quote described the programme as 'voyeuristic, exploitative and degrading, although it has to be said that it also has its bad points'.

Whatever else is said about *Big Brother*, it offers an insight into how people relate to each other. The situation is false, and the fact that the contestants know that their every move is being watched must slant their words and actions. But for all that, I get the feeling when I tune in that I am looking at a large mirror.

Nick may have acted like a rat, but don't we all do the same at times? Isn't the anger we feel at his behaviour in part a recognition of our own double standards? Don't we all exaggerate? Haven't all of us said one thing to someone's face and something else behind their back?

And didn't Jesus say something about those without sin casting the first stone?

Channel 4 getting religious? Excuse me, I think I need to lie down.

For further reading

2 SAMUEL 12:1–10

How would David have reacted if Nathan had come to him and confronted him explicitly with the sinfulness of what he had done? Would he have tried to justify himself and made excuses? As it was, David condemned himself when he 'burned with anger against the man' who, despite his own great wealth, had taken from the poor man the little that he had (v. 5). How do we react when we hear of the mess another person has made in their life? Do we feel better about ourselves because we're not *that* bad? Or do we feel sad, knowing how tough it can be to struggle with temptation, and how prone to failure we ourselves are? Paul warned the Corinthian Christians, 'If you think you are standing firm, be careful that you don't fall!' (1 Corinthians 10:12). If we are tempted to feel self-righteous over the sin of someone else, we should watch out that, in our complacency, we don't fall into similar sin.

Prayer

Pray for someone you know who has become entangled in sin, that they might turn back to God and know again his forgiveness and acceptance. Ask God if he wants you to reach out in some way to help them do that.

Different perspectives

I have come that they may have life and have it to the full.

JOHN 10:10

School's out for summer and, in the nick of time, the weather seems to have got the message. The sunshine of the past few days has shown the south-west at its best. Here's hoping it continues.

Do you have special memories of childhood summer holidays? Older readers will recall times when a day at the seaside was a rare treat and holidays were spent at home rather than jetting away from it all.

I can recall only one family holiday from childhood. Owing to the nature of my father's work, time together as a family was a rare thing, but I have vivid memories of a week spent on a Devon caravan site. It was a special time for a number of reasons—a time that stands out in my memories of childhood.

Years later, over a meal with my parents, we were discussing holidays. I recalled the week in Brixham and remarked that it was a highlight of my childhood.The conversation came to a full stop and I noticed my parents flashing a few unspoken signals before they both burst out laughing.

They remembered the week, but for very different reasons to mine. It rained every day, the caravan was small and uncomfortable, living on top of each other was unbearable, there was very little to do and they had seriously considered coming home early. But to a small lad of eight, who'd hardly noticed the weather, a tiny caravan was fun, being close together an adventure. Playing on the beach was a treat and I'd wanted the week to go on for ever.

I remember spending what was left of my holiday money on a cheap framed photograph of the site and proudly presenting it to my parents as a memento of a magical time. They couldn't remember the picture, just the nightmare of a holiday quickly to be forgotten and never to be repeated.

Why such contrasting memories? One reason might be that adults approach life with different expectations from children.

Consumerism demands that we consider a fortnight in the Caribbean as better than a day at the zoo. But happiness and fulfilment have little to do with surroundings and more to do with the quality of relationships. It doesn't matter where you are so much as who you're with—and that was what made a wet week in Brixham so memorable for one little boy.

For further reading

TITUS 3:3–8

When we have a relationship with God, it changes the way we see things. We are no longer 'enslaved by all kinds of passions and pleasures' (v. 3) but have been set free to enjoy the abundant life that God has planned for us. That is not to say that the Christian life is an easy one or that we will never have another problem. The difference is that we do not face life alone but with the presence and the enabling of the Holy Spirit (vv. 5–6). We may go through difficult times and we may not always feel that God is close by, even though he is. But we have the promise that 'in all things God works for the good of those who love him, who have been called according to his purpose' (Romans 8:28). Therefore we can expect that God will redeem the bad things and the hard things that happen to us and weave them into his beautiful and perfect plan for our lives.

Prayer

O Joy, that seekest me through pain,
I cannot close my heart to Thee;
I trace the rainbow through the rain,
and feel the promise is not vain
That morn shall tearless be.

GEORGE MATHESON (1842–1906)

Do it now

A man's life does not consist in the abundance of his possessions.
LUKE 12:15

'Procrastination is the thief of time.' At least, that's what I remember being told at a tender age when I hadn't got a clue what procrastination meant in the first place. Older, wiser (well, at least able to use a dictionary), I now understand that it means to put off something until later, coming from a Latin word which means 'to postpone until tomorrow'. And those fun-loving Romans certainly knew something about that.

The old proverb came to mind last week when I read about the planned formation of the Procrastinators' Club of Great Britain. Those concerned have been thinking about it for some time... and they plan to go on thinking about it for a little bit longer. Eventually they hope to get around to launching the club and inviting us all to join. Perhaps.

Apparently there is already an American branch of the movement. They are active (gently active, you understand) in promoting their values. On joining, you receive a membership certificate adorned with the club logo—an hourglass with a knot tied in it—bearing the motto, 'We're behind you all the way!' The certificate authorizes a member to 'arrive late, to send out Christmas cards in January, to delay payment of bills and to display this licence conspicuously whenever he (or she) gets around to it.'

I hope they get around to launching the club soon—or soon-ish, as I can think of several friends I'd love to enrol as a surprise gift. Truth to tell, if they ran a procrastination audit, most of us would qualify for a lifetime's free membership.

Why are we so adept at putting things off? Returning library books, cutting the grass, tackling the ironing, filing a tax return, completing a piece of work, making an appointment to see the doctor, talking to your partner, sorting out your relationship with God—just a brief selection of some of the things we delay, with dramatically different consequences: a fine, an overgrown jungle, no shirt for the party, a frosty letter from HM Inspector, the sack, the devastating news that it's too late for treatment, a divorce, an eternity separated from God.

A large part of my job is helping people to understand that neglecting a right relationship with God is not on the same level as getting your library books back a few days late. It is the most important relationship we can cultivate. That is what makes sense of a statement of Jesus that is often quoted. 'What good will it be for a man if he gains the whole world, yet forfeits his soul?' (Matthew 16:26).

The soul is the part of us that lives for ever. Jesus warns about the danger of concentrating on the material at the expense of the spiritual. It's a warning worth taking on board and doing something about—not tomorrow—today.

For further reading

Luke 12:13–21

A huge, unruly crowd had gathered to hear Jesus. Someone in the crowd called out, 'Teacher, tell my brother to divide the inheritance with me' (v. 13). Jesus refused and instead told a parable which warned against the error of believing that 'we are what we have'. The parable described a man who had put all his thought and energy into preparing for a comfortable early retirement. As he had prospered, he had kept everything for himself, storing it in increasingly bigger barns. Unfortunately for him, his efforts were in vain because he did not live to enjoy his wealth and leisure. Worse still, he had ignored God and had not stored up for himself any lasting 'treasure in heaven' (12:33). God does not want us to be preoccupied with making this life comfortable, nor does he want us to worry about whether we shall have enough to live on (12:22). We have this promise: 'Seek his kingdom, and these things will be given to you as well' (12:31).

Prayer

More of thy presence, Lord, impart,
More of thine image let me bear;
Erect thy throne within my heart,
And reign without a rival there.

JOHN NEWTON (1725–1807)

Even the oldest tree

Wisdom is more precious than rubies.
PROVERBS 8:11

A couple who had been married for 50 years were enjoying a quiet evening at home.

'Things have really changed,' the wife said. 'You used to sit next to me on the sofa.'

'I can remedy that,' said the husband, moving next to her.

'And you used to cuddle me,' she said.

'How's that?' he asked as he gave her a tender hug.

The wife smiled. 'Do you remember how you used to drive me wild by nibbling my neck?' she asked. The husband got up to leave the room. 'Where are you going?' his puzzled wife asked.

'I'm off upstairs to fetch my teeth,' he replied.

Sadly, we live in a world that seems obsessed by sell-by dates, but the truth is that even if things aren't exactly the way they once were, it doesn't mean that they are less valuable.

History tells us that some of the greatest achievements have been made by those who had passed official retirement age. For example, the Earl of Halsburg was 90 when he began work on his massive 20-volume revision of English law; Goethe wrote *Faust* at the age of 82; Galileo made his greatest discovery when he was 73.

Many cultures in the world honour those who are old and recognize that with their advancing years comes greater wisdom. They are respected and their advice is sought and heeded. As the book of Proverbs expresses it, 'The glory of young men is their strength, grey hair the splendour of the old' (Proverbs 20:29).

Some of us wish our own society valued age like that, but perhaps part of the answer lies in our own attitude. By living usefully we prove our usefulness.

The Victorian poet Henry Longfellow captured the challenge perfectly in these words:

> *Shall we sit idly down and say,*
> *The night hath come; it is no longer day?*
> *The night hath not yet come; we are not quite*
> *Cut off from labour by the failing light;*
> *Something remains for us to do or dare;*
> *Even the oldest tree some fruit may bear.*

For further reading

1 KINGS 12:1–24

King Solomon's son, Rehoboam, had succeeded him as king. The people of Israel had become increasingly unhappy under Solomon's rule and now they came to Rehoboam, hoping that the new reign would bring a lightening of the burden of taxation and labour. Wisely, the new king asked for time to make a decision and went for advice to 'the elders who had served his father'. But the elders didn't say what he wanted to hear so, unwisely, he turned to friends who were as inexperienced as he was. They rashly advised a crackdown on the people of Israel, and Rehoboam followed their advice, with the consequence that he had to beat a hasty retreat and saw his kingdom diminish in size with only the tribe of Judah submitting to his rule. We sometimes go to other people for advice, hoping that they will tell us what we have already decided to do. At times people give the advice they think is desired rather than saying what they really think. If we are going to seek advice at all we should choose carefully whom we go to, and should look at what they say objectively and prayerfully.

Prayer

Thank you, Lord, for the wisdom that comes from experience. Help me to listen to and learn from those who have known you longer than I have.

Wearing hats in church

God does not show favouritism but accepts men from every nation who fear him and do what is right.

ACTS 10:34–35

It will never catch on as an advert: 'We're the bank that likes to say yes—but only if your face fits!'

If you missed the gaffe of the week, let me recap. A well-known high street bank held a training session for staff, and spelt out that certain types of business customer were not to be welcomed. In particular, taxi drivers and market traders were singled out for the exclusion zone.

The news leaked and there were red faces all round—bank officials at having to defend their policy, and market traders and taxi drivers whose faces were red for a different reason.

Like most things in life, there is an explanation of sorts. The bank in question has difficulty handling cash that is paid in over the counter, and the groups that are to be discouraged tend to deal in loose change, so their business is not welcome.

All of this set me thinking about George Carey's mum. Bear with me as I explain the link. Our soon-to-be-retired Archbishop of Canterbury grew up in a working-class home in the East End of London. When he got involved in his local church as a teenager, he tried to get his parents to go along with him. His mother, although interested, always offered the same excuse for her refusal to attend: she didn't have a hat—and in those post-war days, wearing a hat in church was a very big deal.

George Carey was greatly affected by her decision and determined in his work as a minister to make any church accessible to everyone. No one should feel they couldn't attend because they somehow didn't fit the mould.

In the spirit of 'let him who is without sin cast the first stone', I am anxious to turn the spotlight on churches rather than banks. Jesus, it seems, scandalized his very religious and proper world by making an open offer to *anyone* to follow him. Even worse, he ate and drank with disreputable types and made them his friends. So it follows that his Church should be a place for everyone, with no exclusions. 'Accessible to all' is a brilliant, yet challenging vision.

By the way, taxi drivers, market traders and ladies without hats are especially welcome—and we even accept loose change.

For further reading

Acts 10:9–35

The apostle Peter's first sermon was preached to 'God-fearing Jews from every nation under heaven' (Acts 2:5). When 3,000 of them responded to the message of salvation, he could have been forgiven for thinking that Christianity was limited to the Jewish community. Today it might seem the other way round. It is easy to forget that the Christian faith began with the Jews and a Jewish Messiah. Peter had been so moulded by his upbringing that when God sent a vision to him, he had to have it repeated three times to drive the point home. Peter didn't have to puzzle for very long over the application of what he had seen, because almost immediately he was summoned to the home of a non-Jew, Cornelius the centurion, who had seen a vision of his own. We can become so used to our prejudices, and the distinctions we make between people, that we end up unaware of them. We need to be open to God's challenge to our ingrained ways of thinking. When Jesus died for the world he didn't make any exceptions, and nor should we.

Prayer

Help me, Lord Jesus, to see the people around me as you see them. If the way I think needs to change, make me teachable.

Doorways to Truth

Acting on the facts

Written in October 2001

Jesus answered, 'I am the way and the truth and the life.'
JOHN 14:6

Are women better drivers than men? Far be it from me to disrupt harmony in the home this weekend, but it is an important question. Before reading further, ask yourself for your instinctive answer.

Done it? Then be prepared for a smug grin/nasty shock as appropriate. It seems that women *are* better drivers than men and, what is more, the Advertising Standards Authority has made a ruling this week that supports that opinion.

It stemmed from a complaint against an insurance company that ran a witty advert claiming that women were a better insurance risk than men. The complaint said that this was unfair and the facts did not support such a claim. The insurers did their homework and produced a compelling stack of evidence showing that they were not indulging in advertising hype.

The evidence revealed that women have fewer accidents, make smaller claims and are an all-round better bargain for insurance companies. As far as the ASA are concerned, it's an established fact that women are better drivers than men.

A sense of self-preservation prevents me from saying anything else on the subject, other than to note that I have a male friend who was out in the car with his children recently when the youngest piped up, 'Daddy, before you met Mummy, who told you how to drive?' And now it appears, statistically at least, she has every right to.

There has been much discussion about the need for evidence to support the current international campaign against terrorism, particularly to ensure that the right people are pursued and punished. That is right, and the fact that our own government has shared information (some of which is classified) with leaders of the main opposition parties and secured their support for military involvement says much about the strength of the case.

It was Hiram Johnson, in a speech to the US Senate in 1917, who famously remarked, 'The first casualty when war comes is truth.' But in our information age and under the priceless legacy of democratic government, truth need not be a casualty. A free press and elected representation provide vital checks and balances that previous generations could not even have dreamt of.

Without wishing to be trivial, the ASA ruling this week underlines the difference between fact and opinion. And in all things, both great and small, it is always wisest to act on facts.

For further reading

MATTHEW 27:11–26

Jesus stood before Pilate charged by the religious leaders with 'inciting the people to rebellion' and opposing 'the payment of taxes to Caesar' (Luke 23:2, 14). Pilate, as the Roman governor, would have been obliged to investigate these charges rather than the charge of blasphemy (Matthew 26:65). Jesus could have defended himself but he didn't; he 'made no reply, not even to a single charge' (27:14). If he had, he would have declared the truth—that he was innocent. Instead he accepted the charges just as he accepted the weight of the sin of the world and bore the punishment for it all. Pilate was well aware that Jesus had committed no crime (Luke 23:22) but he was afraid to act on the facts because of the political consequences and the anger of the crowd. The great irony is that he released the man who was guilty of the very crimes Jesus was charged with, and handed an innocent man over to be killed.

Prayer

Lord, when you hung on the cross you were paying the price for my sin. I do not deserve your forgiveness or your love but you give them freely and generously to me. I worship you.

And the good news is...

Written on 21 August 1999

For God so loved the world that he gave his one and only Son, that whoever believes in him shall not perish but have eternal life.
JOHN 3:16

On a warm day in the depths of rural France, I gave in to temptation.

I admit I'm a total news freak. Radio, television and newspapers have made me a junkie for news. When I am on holiday I try to kick the habit, or at least go on a diet, but the sight of a fat, English, Sunday paper enticing me from the news-stand was too much to bear. So I gave in and settled down at a pavement café for my fix, like an escapee from a health farm facing a mountain of junk food. It was bliss with a capital B and several s's.

Two stories caught my eye—the first, a report of an interview with America's first lady, Hilary Clinton, and the second, an article announcing Microsoft founder Bill Gates' decision to give away millions of dollars to charitable projects in the Third World.

The stories probably did me more good than a sermon. Hilary Clinton was asked about her husband's much publicized weaknesses and gave a robust line of reasoning as to her abilities both to understand and deal with them. She was asked about her personal Christian faith and its ability to withstand such severe testing. She cited Peter's famous denial of Jesus and how the power of love not only makes forgiveness a possibility but opens the door for the forgiven individual to find a way to change.

Bill Gates and his wife have spent some of their massive fortune travelling the world, including the shanty towns of Africa and Asia. Confronted by the massive threat of AIDS and other epidemics, they decided to plough millions of dollars into a wide variety of health projects in the poorest countries of the world.

It didn't take more than five minutes for my cynicism glands to kick in (they were on holiday too, so they were slower than usual in responding). Hilary is ambitious for office and is likely to run as Senator for New York. The interview is a calculated spin on her slighted yet forgiving persona that is bound to pull votes. And for Gates, arguably the world's richest man, his donations are the sort of small change he would hardly notice.

But just for a few minutes on a sunny day in France I caught myself wanting to believe in some plain, no-nonsense human goodness—goodness for goodness' sake.

For further reading

ISAIAH 61:1–2; LUKE 4:14–30

Before the days of newspapers, Isaiah the prophet and others like him were announcing forthcoming events so far in the future that they would not live to see them happen. Jesus' statement in Luke leaves us in no doubt that Isaiah was talking about him: 'Today this scripture is fulfilled in your hearing' (v. 21). What good news! But, amazingly, the people of Nazareth did not respond to this with pleasure and excitement. They could not see beyond the fact that Jesus was the local carpenter's son to the possibility that he might be the long-awaited Messiah. In fact, they were so 'furious' that they tried to kill Jesus—not the usual response to good news! Many people today look for good news in the wrong places. They look at the church or at Christians and stop there; they don't look at Jesus. If they did, they would see that 'God so loved the world that he gave his one and only Son, that whoever believes in him shall not perish but have eternal life' (John 3:16). And that is good news that we can believe wholeheartedly.

Prayer

Thank you, Lord, that the good news about Jesus is utterly reliable.

Also by Ian Coffey with Kim Bush

Windows on the World from the Word

This companion volume to *Doorways from the Word to the World* is for all of us who want to connect our everyday lives with Bible teaching—but who don't feel we have enough time to do it. Ideal for use on a daily, weekly or occasional basis, it offers 'God thoughts' on issues in today's world, showing how Christian faith can be 'earthed' in the reality of the challenges and situations that each of us, in different ways, have to face. Comments are linked to Bible passages and conclude with a prayer or thought for reflection, and each piece is short enough to read through in ten minutes!

ISBN 1 84101 149 5   £6.99

Available from your local Christian bookshop or direct from BRF using the order form on page 207.

***** **Also from BRF** *****

On This Rock

Bible foundations for Christian living

Stephen Cottrell

'As you read this book I hope you will learn to love the Bible, and be excited by its claims and challenges. But, more importantly, I hope you will be led closer to Jesus.'

Stephen Cottrell has written this book for new Christians who want to grow in their faith and for more experienced Christians who want to re-set the compass of their discipleship. In 28 Bible readings telling the story of the apostle Peter, he explores what being a disciple meant back then, and how it relates to the life of a disciple today. As well as teaching about how to grow as a follower of Jesus, the book will help establish a regular pattern for Bible reading, reflection and prayer.

ISBN 1 84101 238 6   £3.99

Available from your local Christian bookshop or direct from BRF using the order form on page 207.

Urban God

Bible readings and comment on living in the city

John Proctor

Urban God combs the Bible for stories about cities, and finds many echoes between Bible times and city living today. The Bible speaks well of urban life, and of how good it can be with God. There is plenty of realism, too, about what a mess a city can be without God. In cities, like everywhere else, human life is mixed material: made by God, marred by our mistakes, and yet constantly beckoned to the promise of God's renewing love. God believes in cities—but it also matters that cities believe in God.

So read God's story in the Bible, and hold it alongside your own. Let scripture teach you more of what God sees, enjoys and longs for in your place. And read the Bible with sharper eyes, because the God you meet in its pages is the God you serve in the days and duties of your own life.

ISBN 1 84101 256 4   £5.99

Available from your local Christian bookshop or direct from BRF using the order form on page 207.

The Subversive Manifesto

Lifting the lid on God's political agenda

Jonathan Bartley

God has a political agenda—and it's a subversive one, according to this book which lays down a radical challenge for Christians to rediscover the political dimension of their faith. All too often we stick with 'private' readings of scripture, failing to realize the power contained in its amazing stories and ideas. In fact the Bible presents a faith that is wider and more exciting than we realize—a faith that can change not only people's hearts but also the way societies are run, economies are structured, and legal systems organized.

With illustrations drawn from the author's experiences in the 'corridors of power', this book combines an innovative interpretation of the Bible with challenging ideas for applying it to everyday life.

ISBN 1 84101 211 4   £7.99

Available from your local Christian bookshop or direct from BRF using the order form on page 207.

ORDER FORM

REF	TITLE	PRICE	QTY	TOTAL
149 5	*Windows on the World from the Word*	£6.99		
238 6	*On This Rock*	£3.99		
256 4	*Urban God*	£5.99		
211 4	*The Subversive Manifesto*	£7.99		

POSTAGE AND PACKING CHARGES

order value	UK	Europe	Surface	Air Mail
£7.00 & under	£1.25	£3.00	£3.50	£5.50
£7.01–£30.00	£2.25	£5.50	£6.50	£10.00
Over £30.00	free	prices on request		

Postage and packing:

Donation:

Total enclosed:

Name _____ Account Number _____

Address _____

_____ Postcode _____

Telephone Number _____ Email _____

Payment by: Cheque ❑ Mastercard ❑ Visa ❑ Postal Order ❑ Switch ❑

Credit card no. ☐☐☐☐ ☐☐☐☐ ☐☐☐☐ ☐☐☐☐   Expires ☐☐ ☐☐

Switch card no. ☐☐☐☐☐☐☐☐☐☐☐☐☐☐☐☐☐☐

Issue no. of Switch card ☐☐☐☐   Expires ☐☐ ☐☐

Signature _____ Date _____

All orders must be accompanied by the appropriate payment.

Please send your completed order form to:
BRF, First Floor, Elsfield Hall, 15–17 Elsfield Way, Oxford OX2 8FG
Tel. 01865 319700 / Fax. 01865 319701 Email: enquiries@brf.org.uk

❑ Please send me further information about BRF publications.

Available from your local Christian bookshop.   **BRF is a Registered Charity**